Black Magic Academy

Emily Martha Sorensen

Also by Emily Martha Sorensen

Comics:

A Magical Roommate
(available online)

To Prevent World Peace
(available in-print or online)

Black Magic Academy
Copyright © 2012 by Emily Martha Sorensen
Cover image by Mandy Roberts

All rights reserved. Printed in the United States of America.

ISBN: 978-1-949607-37-6

http://www.emilymarthasorensen.com

To Ms. Robillard,
my tenth-grade English teacher,
who taught me how to write a query letter.

To Ben,
my wonderful, beloved husband.

To all my readers,
whose love makes this work possible.

Chapter 1
Captives and Cabbage

"ood news!" Aunt Anklistine strode into the kitchen, rubbing her hands. Her hair was pulled back in its usual severe bun, wisps trailing out at the ends. Her angular face looked gleeful. "Someone stole a cabbage from our garden!"

Aunt Lilith squinted up from the cauldron she was stirring. She brushed her spotless apron and dipped a finger in the boiling liquid to taste the brew. "A cabbage? Already?"

Aunt Anklistine flicked at her boots. Caked mud clumped off and landed by the doormat. "Yes, already. They've been enchanted since yesterday. I told you my lures work quickly."

Mildred looked up from the squirming orange mash she was supposed to be chopping for dinner tonight. It looked atrocious and smelled repulsive. Probably Aunt Hurda's idea of dessert. *Good news that someone stole from us?* she wondered.

Aunt Lilith sighed. "You realize we don't have a room free to keep a captive yet."

"Oh, we can use Mildred's." Aunt Anklistine ran her bony fingers through her hair. "She won't need it much longer. Once she leaves —"

"Excuse me?" Mildred burst in.

Aunt Lilith jumped, looking guilty.

"I thought she was banned from the kitchen." Aunt Anklistine frowned at the corner where Mildred had sat hidden. "Doesn't she burn everything?"

"She's not stirring, she's chopping. Besides, she has to learn to cook eventually."

"What a nuisance," Aunt Anklistine muttered.

"Mildred's not a nuisance! There's every chance she'll grow up to be just as creditable as her mother. Besides, Drakin was . . ."

Evil? Vicious? Vindictive? No loss to anybody? Mildred thought sourly.

". . . irreplaceable," Aunt Lilith finished. "But our niece has her own qualities —"

"Such as trying to talk to *Normals?*"

Mildred's face turned hot. *One* time she'd tried to sneak out of the manor to find a friend. *Once.* Why couldn't Aunt Anklistine let her forget it?

Aunt Lilith sighed. "Be that as it may . . . you realize that if we leave to fetch the thief, we'll have to take Hurda with us. That was Oplisa's condition for letting us out for the day."

Aunt Anklistine's face pinched. "I suppose she might have some use . . ."

Mildred sighed. Aunt Oplisa saw it as her duty to coerce the middle sisters to include the youngest, but she rarely subjected herself to Aunt Hurda personally.

The front door slammed, and both aunts stiffened.

Aunt Hurda stomped into the kitchen. Her clothes were coated in mud and grass stains. Her favorite necklace of cockroach legs was knocked askew, and her right foot trailed a cobweb with brambles tangled in it.

"Got a cabbage missing," she grunted.

"I know that. I planted them." Aunt Anklistine folded her arms. "Unless two are missing because you just ate one?"

"What did you wear into *my* kitchen?" Aunt Lilith screamed. "Get out! Get out! Take that filth with you!"

Ignoring her, Aunt Hurda dipped her knuckle in the stew and slurped. "Not burnt enough yet." She knelt down by the fire and blew. The flames roared.

Aunt Lilith wrenched her sister away. *"Get out of my kitchen!"*

Mildred tried not to giggle.

Aunt Hurda didn't seem to notice. She reached out and snagged a handful of squirming orange mash.

"No good raw." She shoved it in her mouth anyway. "Burn it, too."

"I've told you before," Aunt Lilith said through gritted teeth. "Stay out of my kitchen twelve nights a week, and you get to cook the thirteenth. Why is that so difficult to remember?"

"Once a week not enough," Aunt Hurda mumbled through her mouthful. "Don't get enough respect as it is."

Aunt Anklistine's eyebrows drew together. "Well, if someone hadn't refused to declare a death-enemy when she came of age . . ."

"Nobody I wanted to kill," Aunt Hurda shot back.

"That isn't actually necessary," Aunt Lilith snapped, snatching the remainder of the orange mash from the counter and squishing it into a bowl. "I've never killed a witch in my life."

Mildred nodded. Very few witches took the term literally. Aunt Anklistine competed with her enemy to make nastier gardens. Aunt Lilith stole recipes from hers. Of course, Aunt Oplisa had killed her death-enemy years ago, but Aunt Oplisa killed everything.

"Speaking of which," Aunt Anklistine said pointedly, "don't we have a Normal to go out and capture?"

"Oh! Right. Right." Aunt Lilith snapped her fingers, and the fire under the pot died. She smacked Aunt Hurda's hand away from her shelf of alphabetized cookbooks, and said, reluctantly, "Would you like to come with us?"

Aunt Hurda grinned, showing her black teeth. "I like capturing things."

Aunt Lilith's shoulders slumped. "Go to your room, Mildred," she said morosely. "Clean it out. We'll be back in an hour."

"But I need my room!" Mildred protested. "It's small and private and has the best view in the manor —"

"Towers are traditional for keeping captives," Aunt Anklistine snapped. "Stop arguing and do it."

"Then where am I supposed to sleep?" Mildred cried.

"You can have Drakin's old room," Aunt Lilith said kindly, as if offering a generous gift.

Mildred stared at her in horror.

"I'll cook tonight," Aunt Hurda offered, pulling a limp ball of fur from her pocket. "Rat soup."

"ABSOLUTELY *NOT!*" Aunt Lilith screamed, diving to stop her.

Mildred slammed the door to her room. How dare they take it away! And to give it to some prisoner! And now they wanted her to sleep in Drakin's horrible bedroom . . .

Mildred shuddered. Drakin had been dead since she was two or three, too young to remember. But she hated hearing the stories about her mother. Drakin had been worse than Aunt Oplisa, manipulating people's minds instead of just killing things.

Mildred sighed, flipping through her closet dispiritedly. *Of course, it isn't like I have much to take with me.*

Three dresses that still fit. Several piles of ones that didn't. A few forgotten toys from when she was much younger, which had collected dust for years. Spellbooks . . .

Oh! Mildred's eyes widened. She yanked back a pile of too-small dresses back to find a stack of old, forgotten books from the family library. Histories of the kingdom from two hundred years ago, heroes who defeated witches, princesses with perfectly golden hair . . . Aunt Anklistine had long-since threatened to burn those if she caught Mildred reading any more of "that trash."

Teetering under a stack of twelve tomes, Mildred inched down the stairs and stumbled her way to the library. She scanned the bookcases, finally spying a top shelf that wasn't quite full. Breathing a sigh of relief, Mildred dragged over a chair and hid them all behind the spellbooks in the front row, which had titles like *Deadly Poisons in Your Garden*, *Famous Feuds of the Last Thousand Years*, and *Leave Your Enemies Helpless*.

She jumped down from the chair and squinted upwards. Good. You couldn't tell from here that anything had changed. That should save her from a scolding, unless Aunt Lilith took inventory again.

Running back up the stairs, she flicked through the rest of her possessions, which didn't take long.

Spellbooks. They could keep those. She rarely read them, anyway.

Slippers. She tucked them in her pocket.

Clothes. Mildred stared dismally at her wardrobe. Two of her dresses were threadbare, one was just plain ugly, and she'd never liked that blue cloak. *Maybe if I leave them here, they'll get the hint that I need something new.*

Mildred eyed her mattress uncertainly. Possibly, if she dragged that downstairs, they might let her sleep in the kitchen instead of Drakin's old room . . .

"— *Your* fault it nearly got away!"

Mildred jumped. *Aunt Anklistine!*

"Stop yelling!" Aunt Lilith shouted back. "It didn't get away, did it? Hurda, stop letting it struggle so much!"

The door exploded. Aunt Hurda appeared in a cloud of dust, tossing the front end of a screaming, wriggling sack at the mattress.

"MMFHFHH MHFFMNMM MFHHHMMMN!" the sack shouted.

Mildred stared at it, dumbfounded.

"Too heavy," Aunt Hurda muttered, kicking the back half onto the mattress. It yelped and started swearing at her. "Room all ready?"

Mildred nodded nervously.

Aunt Lilith appeared at the top of her stairs, her face red and beaded with sweat. She glared at the sack and marched straight to Mildred's window, gasping for breath as she squinted down the side of the wall. "High enough to . . . keep it contained . . . you think?"

"Meh," Aunt Hurda grunted, peering over her shoulder.

Aunt Anklistine shoved Aunt Hurda aside and looked outside. "Not nearly high enough," she said crisply. "It might survive a fall from this distance. Let's use something else to keep it in."

Aunt Lilith raised her fingers from the windowsill and stared at them, looking disgusted. "Mildred, this place is filthy. There must be a week of dust here. Don't you ever clean it?"

"Too clean already," Aunt Hurda muttered, pulling a sack of grey powder out of a pocket and dumping it across the floor. "That's better."

Aunt Lilith shrieked in outrage.

Aunt Anklistine pulled off one of her sharp-heeled boots. "Mildred, get my flameberry seeds."

Mildred was still watching the writhing sack. "Which seeds?"

"Flameberry," Aunt Anklistine said coldly. "Relative of poison ivy? Top drawer of my seed cabinet, left side?"

"Oh. Right." Mildred tore her eyes away. "You're . . . you're not going to hurt the Normal, are you?"

Aunt Hurda pulled a picture from the wall and put it back upside-down.

Aunt Anklistine removed the other sharp-heeled boot. "Would you rather be included in the hurting?"

Mildred gulped. The heels of those shoes hurt. She knew because Aunt Anklistine had thrown them at her last week.

"The correct answer is 'no,' of course," Aunt Lilith directed, snatching the picture and turning it rightside-up again. "So you might want to hurry."

Mildred raced down the stairs, narrowly avoiding tripping on the loose step. She hurried down the shabby hallway. Aunt Anklistine's room was the third door down, halfway between Aunt Hurda's pigsty and the macabre bedroom that had once been Drakin's.

Aunt Anklistine's room was covered with clutter, bags of fertilizer, and gardening tools. The seed cabinet took up three full walls — there was barely enough space left for the mattress shoved in a corner — and it was so crammed full that when she yanked the right drawer open, several drawstring bags poured out and spilled their contents across the floor.

Mildred winced. She hoped Aunt Anklistine could remember which of those tiny brown seeds were which.

The flameberry bag was labeled, fortunately. She pulled the fireproof pouch out carefully and tucked it in her pocket. Then she ran back up the stairs again.

Aunt Hurda was grinding one of Mildred's dresses into the floor while Aunt Lilith pulled a cobweb from the ceiling, looking repulsed.

"Flameberry seeds," Mildred panted, holding out the pouch.

"Took long enough," Aunt Anklistine snapped, grabbing it from her. "Hurda, get over here! I need you to activate these."

Aunt Hurda didn't look up from the petticoat she was scrubbing with dust. "Do it yourself."

"I'm an *earth witch!*" Aunt Anklistine shouted.

"Oh, *I'll* do it," Aunt Lilith said, snatching the seed bag. "What do you need?"

"Just wake them. I'll grow them."

"Fine." Aunt Lilith poured seeds into her left hand. They were round and red, and ridged like tiny pumpkins. She picked up each one in turn, blew on it, and it burst into flames. Then she dropped it out the window. Each one exploded as it hit the ground.

"Good. Thirteen," Aunt Anklistine said, taking the pouch back. She tied the drawstring around her wrist. "What do you think? Just straight up, or around the whole tower?"

"Up and around," Aunt Lilith said. "And thatched if you want them to look ornamental."

Aunt Anklistine grunted and began to trace lines in the air with her fingers. She pulled a bag of fertilizer from her pocket and emptied it down on the seeds.

"FLAMEBERRIES, GROW!" she shouted.

For a moment, nothing happened. Then flameberry vines exploded through the window, across the wall, and all down the floor.

Mildred leapt back as a cluster of berries roared past her.

"Unhealthy," Aunt Anklistine said critically, picking up one of the vines and frowning at it. "Insufficient nutrients. That's the problem with these mass-growing spells. But it'll have to do."

"Should we let . . . *it* out now?" Aunt Lilith asked, wrinkling her nose.

Aunt Hurda upended the sack. A disheveled Normal girl dumped out onto the floor.

A girl. Mildred felt a mixture of relief and disappointment. She'd seen men from a distance, but she'd never spoken with one, not really. Aunt Lilith scolded her whenever she tried to talk to Normals, and Aunt Oplisa didn't let male witches near the manor.

The captive crawled to a sitting position and glared up at them through her mass of tangled hair. She looked mean, and too skinny to be healthy. There was also a long scar down her face.

"I HATE YOU ALL!" she shouted.

"We ought to give it a name," Aunt Lilith said, wiping her fingertips along a closet shelf and shuddering at the traces of dust she found. "Thoughts, Anklistine?"

"Cabbage," Aunt Hurda grinned, showing off rotten teeth.

Aunt Anklistine considered. "Cabbage it is."

"That's NOT my name!" the girl shouted. "It's *Beauty!*"

Aunt Lilith stared at her incredulously. Aunt Hurda snickered.

The girl glared. "I wasn't born with this scar."

Aunt Anklistine yawned. "Just tell it why it's here, Lilith."

Aunt Lilith frowned. "Very well. Cabbage —"

"*Beauty —*"

"— You're here because you stole something from us. That means we get to keep you here as long as we want."

The girl scowled. "It does not."

"Does so," Aunt Lilith sniffed. "There's even a law about it. If you can't return the object you stole, or another in kind —"

The girl's eyes darted side-to-side. She looked worried.

"— We're entitled to keep you in debtors' prison until the debt is paid."

"Bet it ate the cabbage," Aunt Hurda noted, looking pleased.

"Of course it did; no one would steal from a witch's garden unless they were starving," Aunt Anklistine said impatiently. "No matter how appetizing the lure spells planted."

"So," Aunt Lilith finished, "we can keep you here as long as we like. I doubt you have family; we own all the land in this area; we've been legally wronged; and the village is afraid of us, anyway. Nobody's coming to rescue you. Nobody cares."

The girl's eyes flicked fearfully around the room. "Then why don't you just kill me?"

"Isn't it obvious?" Aunt Lilith purred. "We want a prisoner."

"Though we *might* kill you if you try to escape," Aunt Anklistine snorted.

"And in the meantime . . ." Aunt Lilith stopped, shuddering. "Hurda's going to cook all your food."

Aunt Hurda grinned. "Finally, my own time in the kitchen."

"Trust me," Aunt Lilith said fervently, "you might wish you were dead."

Chapter 2

Revelations

ildred woke up to a horrible stench. She opened her eyes to see Aunt Hurda's face.

"Wh-wh-wh-what do you want?" Mildred yelped, scrambling to pull a blanket over her nose.

Aunt Hurda grabbed her wrists. "I want to tell you the truth," she hissed. "Before Oplisa gets home."

Mildred struggled not to inhale. Her aunt's breath stank.

"H-here?" she gasped out. "N-now? About what?"

Aunt Hurda grinned. "About Drakin," she said. "You want to know, don't you?"

"A-about what?" Mildred scrunched the blanket around her nose, hoping it would help slightly. It didn't. "What are you talking about?"

"Drakin." Aunt Hurda smirked and leaned back. In the dim light, even her torn nightgown seemed ragged and filthy. Mildred hoped that caked mud was illusion. "You want to know why your mother died, don't you? Who your father was?"

Mildred's heart skipped a beat. She forgot about her aunt's breath. "You're going to *tell* me?" she gasped.

Aunt Hurda looked gleeful. "You ever heard of Welsa?"

Mildred racked her brain. "Noooooo," she said uncertainly.

"Drakin's death-enemy? Purest hatred for each other?"

Mildred shook her head.

"Salutatorian the year they graduated? Always second-best to Drakin?"

Mildred chewed on her lower lip.

Aunt Hurda sighed. "Well, she got sick of it. Challenged Drakin to a death-match. Know about *those,* don't you?"

Mildred gulped and nodded. They were a formal way of killing your death-enemy. Supposedly, they were more prestigious than mere stabs in the back or poisoning. But she'd never heard of anyone actually risking it.

"Wish you could have seen it." Aunt Hurda grinned, showing off her yellow teeth. "Perfectly matched. Intense hatred. Unbridled power. Drakin even won. But Welsa got a parting shot in just as she was dying, so they killed each other." She scowled. "Most annoying. Oplisa's been running our lives ever since."

Mildred's heart pounded. So that was how her mother had died. It explained a lot. "So — what about my father?" she asked hesitantly. "Is he — still alive?"

Aunt Hurda sniffed. "Would we be stuck with you if he were?"

Mildred swallowed. "Well," she said cautiously, "if he was really bad at magic, and you didn't want him raising me to be weak, too . . ."

"Wasn't a witch at all. He was a Normal."

Mildred's eyes widened. "He — *what?*"

"Oplisa doesn't want you to know," Aunt Hurda hissed, leaning in closer. "Thinks it would be a big distraction. You can't let on I told you."

"But — but why would Drakin *marry* him?" Mildred burst out. "That makes no sense! Unless — unless . . ." She swallowed, a question on the tip of her tongue that she'd always wanted to ask. "Did Drakin . . . did she love my father?"

Aunt Hurda let out a shriek of laughter. She almost fell to the ground, she was laughing so hard.

"Drakin — *love?*" she gasped. "Whatever gave you *that* idea?"

Mildred shrank back, feeling close to tears. "Well — well, I thought — maybe —"

"Look," Aunt Hurda sneered, "Drakin never loved. Not her sisters. Not her daughter. Certainly no Normal man."

Mildred tried to swallow the lump in her throat.

"Then . . . then why?" she whispered.

Aunt Hurda shrugged. "Wanted to test her latest love spell.

Lifetime dedication, all that. And *you* were a mistake. That's why she left you with Lilith. She never cared about *you*."

Tears welled up in Mildred's eyes. So even her mother hadn't wanted her. Even her horrible mother . . .

"But there's more you should know," Aunt Hurda hissed. "Welsa was married too. She —"

"Mildred!"

Mildred jumped to see Aunt Lilith in the doorway.

Aunt Hurda coughed and slid off Mildred's quilt, leaving a trail of grime. Her eyes shifted around, looking guilty. "Just thought someone should say —"

Aunt Lilith didn't even bother to look at her. "Oplisa's home, Mildred. She wants to talk to you."

Mildred traced her finger along the grain of the midnight-blue wooden door, reluctant to open it. She hated visiting her least favorite aunt. Screwing up her courage, Mildred pushed the latch aside and creaked it open.

Aunt Oplisa's back was turned to her, tracing runes across a wall of water. "Come in," she said, glancing at Mildred's reflection. "I have news for you."

Mildred shuffled in, swallowing. Had Aunt Anklistine complained about the belladonnas she'd crashed into during her disastrous broomstick lesson last week? Was she going to be punished again?

Oh, no. She hoped this wasn't going to be another of those lectures about why emotions were weakness.

Aunt Oplisa ran her fingers across the water mirror. It rippled. "As you know, I take great interest in your education."

Mildred nodded glumly. That was why she had always received spellbooks, rather than toys or new clothing, every time her aunts gave her anything.

"Do you know where I've been, Drakin's daughter?"

Probably killing another enemy. Mildred shrugged.

Aunt Oplisa smiled. There was the barest hint of warmth in it.

"I've been speaking with Tractia, the High Witch of Black Magic Academy. As you know, your mother was a valedictorian there."

Mildred shrugged.

"Your name has finally reached the top of the waiting list. You'll be starting school tomorrow."

Mildred's eyes widened. *I'll WHAT?*

"This is a moment we have long anticipated." Aunt Oplisa's smile flowed slightly warmer. "I'm sure you'll prove our family worthy of further honors this generation."

"I'm not going!" Mildred burst out.

Aunt Oplisa froze, looking startled.

"I'm not — I'm not — I'm not going! I'm not! I am *not* going there!"

Aunt Oplisa's eyes darkened. "Every member of our family goes to Black Magic Academy."

"Aunt Lilith didn't! And Aunt Hurda —"

Mildred stopped. *Aunt Hurda got kicked out.* Probably not wisest to remind Aunt Oplisa about that.

"Lilith was never accepted in the first place," Aunt Oplisa said frostily. "You have been."

"But," Mildred began desperately.

"You are *Drakin's daughter.*" Aunt Oplisa's eyes flashed. "She was the finest witch of her generation. And you are the *only* member of your generation of our family."

Why can't you just have some children yourself?! Mildred raged. *I don't want to be the only member of my generation of the family!*

"I'm not — going," she repeated stubbornly.

"Of course you are." Aunt Oplisa turned back to the mirror. "The matter is settled."

"No, it isn't!" Mildred shrieked. "I'm not going!"

Aunt Oplisa didn't even glance back. "Don't be foolish, Drakin's daughter. You don't want to make me your enemy."

Her mirror frosted into ice, and shattered. Slivers sprayed across the room and sliced curtains, embedding into the wall.

Mildred went mute.

"Now, do get a few more hours of sleep." Aunt Oplisa waved a hand to dismiss her. "It will make a much better impression tomorrow morning. You exist purely to further our family's glory, Drakin's daughter. Always remember that. There is no other reason."

Chapter 3

The Badge and the Broomstick

"You haven't even tested for her *element* yet?"

Aunt Oplisa's furious voice echoed down the hallway. In it was all the scorn she usually reserved for talking about men.

Mildred's hand jerked away from the latch to the kitchen door. *Maybe I should wait until they've stopped arguing.*

"Not safe . . ." Aunt Lilith's voice mumbled. "Qualified testers need to . . . school's much better-equipped . . ."

"Oh, don't be so squeamish," Aunt Oplisa snorted. "Tests don't have to be *that* life-threatening. Mother nearly drowned me to find out I'm a water witch."

"I'm not going to try to drown my own niece!" Aunt Lilith snarled. "Nor am I going to shove her off a tower or throw her in a fireplace!"

Mildred shivered. The occasional stories she heard about her grandparents were not pleasant. She was glad they had both died before she was born.

"Perhaps I could run some tests myself," Aunt Oplisa mused. "If she sleeps much longer, she'll be too late to start classes this morning, anyway . . ."

Mildred scrambled for the latch and shoved the door open.

"Here I am!" she said hastily.

Aunt Lilith glanced her over. "You look dreadful," she said. "Did you sleep at all?"

Mildred nodded hesitantly. She had managed almost half an hour of sleep.

"Well, clearly it wasn't enough." Aunt Oplisa looked disgusted. "Make her presentable, Lilith."

"Of course!" Aunt Lilith leapt to her feet, looking relieved. "Come with me!"

Mildred cast a longing look at the food on the table: boiled slugs and candied nightshade and pigs' feet and nettle pancakes . . .

"*Mildred!*" Aunt Lilith hissed, seizing her arm.

Reluctantly, Mildred let her drag her out of the kitchen.

"You really ought to wear something less ragged than that," Aunt Lilith murmured as they climbed up the stairs. "That black dress is almost threadbare."

"I'd love to have another one that still fit," Mildred said touchily.

"Ah. Well, can't be helped, then." Aunt Lilith sidestepped the loose stair and touched a crack in the wall as they passed. "Maybe we can darken your blue cloak. That would be something."

"Or you could just turn me invisible instead," Mildred said hopefully. "We could both pretend I went to school, and Aunt Oplisa would never notice —"

Aunt Lilith snorted. "Oplisa would notice."

"You've known all along, haven't you?" Mildred accused. "You should have *told* me I was getting sent there!"

"Seemed imprudent," Aunt Lilith shrugged. "You'd hide."

Mildred glared at her.

Aunt Lilith touched the smooth, polished latch to her door. It slid open to reveal six walls covered in identical shelving. In the center sat a bare mattress. No other furniture, no knickknacks, and very few possessions. What shelves weren't empty were filled with books.

"Let's start with the basics," Aunt Lilith said. She headed for the wall directly opposite them, running her finger along the spines of a hundred or so alphabetized spellbooks. She opened one and started flipping through it. "Dust remover, dust remover . . ."

Grey dirt dumped down on Mildred's head.

Mildred coughed, looked up, and found Aunt Hurda grinning at her. Her usually-black teeth looked yellow today.

Aunt Lilith slammed the book shut. "*Hurda!*"

Aunt Hurda held up a pair of chicken bones. "For her hair."

Aunt Lilith seized the bones and flung them out the window.

Aunt Hurda shrugged, pulled a dead rat from her pocket, and tried to arrange that in Mildred's hair instead.

Aunt Lilith shrieked in outrage and snatched a pair of gloves from the shelf behind her.

"You're not going to use illusion to make my teeth look rotten again, are you?" Mildred asked warily.

Aunt Hurda grinned.

"*Get out!*" Aunt Lilith snarled.

Mildred fought a laugh.

Aunt Lilith yanked the dead rat out of Mildred's hair, sent three cleaning rags whizzing across the floor, and cast several spells to remove Aunt Hurda's dirt. Then she chanted away the dark circles under Mildred's eyes and pulled her hair into a tight bun.

"You're no beauty," Aunt Lilith said critically, finishing a spell to turn Mildred's cloak inky black, "but at least you won't embarrass us."

Two minutes later, Aunt Hurda snuck in and dumped a bag of soot over Mildred's head.

While Aunt Lilith was screaming, Aunt Anklistine strode in.

"Here," she said, holding out a squat badge. "Oplisa said to give this to you."

Mildred took it cautiously. "What does it do?"

Letters appeared on the badge:

Black Magic Academy
Student
Fifth Class

"Put it on," Aunt Anklistine said.

Mildred tried to pull the badge off her hand. It wouldn't budge. She yanked —

Yes! It was off!

Wait. No. It was stuck to her *other* hand.

Mildred scowled.

"You can't get rid of that until you graduate or get expelled," Aunt Anklistine said. "It'll stick to you unless you put it on the clothes you're wearing."

Mildred held her hand over the front of her dress, and the badge leapt onto it. She pulled it off again, fought with it for a moment, and somehow managed to get it stuck to her slippers.

"That was Drakin's badge," Aunt Anklistine said coolly, as Mildred tugged it off and got it stuck to one of her sleeves. "Treat it with respect."

Now it wouldn't come off her elbow!

"Do I have to bring anything else with me?" Mildred asked, fighting to shove the badge back onto her cloak. *Argh!* Now it was stuck to her hair! "Books or spells or, um —"

The badge lodged itself firmly on top of her head.

"Your brains," Aunt Anklistine snapped, "if there are any in that head of yours."

"Is something wrong here?"

Mildred froze as she heard Aunt Oplisa's voice. The badge slid down her hair and attached itself to her cloak.

"Why is she covered in soot?" Aunt Oplisa asked coldly.

Aunt Anklistine gestured while Aunt Lilith chanted; the soot fell to the floor and crumbled to ash.

Aunt Hurda pouted, skulking in the corner.

Aunt Oplisa held out a polished broomstick. "Sit down, Drakin's daughter."

Mildred flinched. "I, um, I'm not so good with brooms . . ."

"So Anklistine's told me." Aunt Oplisa's voice was flat. "I'll control it. Just sit."

Gulping, Mildred obeyed.

Aunt Oplisa gave her an incredulous look. Mildred looked down and saw she'd sat with the bristles behind her.

"Wrong *way?*" Aunt Anklistine said, sounding exasperated.

Face flushing, Mildred turned around so the bristles faced front.

Aunt Oplisa spoke loudly. "Broom! You will take the witch now seated on you to Black Magic Academy. No detours, no stops, no deceleration. Now go!"

The broomstick lurched into the air. Mildred clutched the bristles, which felt even stiffer and scratchier than her mattress.

"Isn't there any other way —" she began desperately.

"*Go!*" Aunt Oplisa ordered, pointing at the window.

The broom shot through it, bolting forward at a breakneck pace. Mildred clung to the handle, cheek pressed against the polished wood, fighting airsickness. She finally forced her eyes open to watch the manor recede into the distance, but it had already vanished.

Mildred swallowed, tears pricking at the edge of her vision. She knew most of her aunts saw it as a prison, but the manor had been her only home.

The sun was setting, and her back was killing her. Her fingers ached from their white-knuckled grip on the broomstick handle, and her mind had gone numb from a mix of boredom, terror, and exhaustion. Trees, trees, trees, endless *trees* . . . all they had flown over for hours was this expanse of trees.

Then she noticed the building.

It lurked like an enormous dragon, deep in the heart of the forest. She thought it *was* a dragon, at first. Light glinted off a few obsidian scales, while the rest seemed to absorb the daylight, sleek and cold and unyielding to the morning rays. The entrance gaped like a mouthful of teeth, waiting . . . waiting to swallow her.

I am not going in there, Mildred decided, gripping the broomstick handle.

"We — we're going to turn around now —" she began, her voice quavering.

SLAM!

The broom smashed into the ground, exploding up clouds of dirt and shoving Mildred's face into a pile of leaves. Coughing and choking, Mildred staggered to her feet, pulling leaves out of her hair and noting dismally that she was now covered in dirt all over again.

"Pitiful," a voice said.

Mildred jerked her head up, startled. A tall, dark-skinned woman was watching from the shadows of the building.

"E-excuse me?" she stammered.

"Pitiful," the woman repeated. "I expected better from Oplisa's niece. But perhaps you'll survive. Come. We'll go to your dorm."

Mildred stared at her, aghast. *Perhaps you'll survive?*

What had her aunts gotten her into?

Chapter 4

Death-Enemies

The entrance yawned like a gigantic mouth, complete with obsidian teeth. Mildred shivered as they walked through it, then shuddered as they headed down the hallway.

Dim candles lit dark walls, but they didn't disguise disguise the shape of the building, nor prevent the strong impression that something was swallowing them.

WHAT were the architects thinking?

Mildred brushed against a leering statue, and stifled a shriek. It felt like it had a pulse.

"Fitting, isn't it?" The High Witch smiled. "Drakin brought them all to life one night. Or perhaps she just set Forest Beyond creatures loose in the halls — we never did figure out which. Of course, we had to put her on probation because she'd broken several rules to do that . . ." High Witch Tractia sighed. "Killing's forbidden on Academy grounds, but she *would* keep trying to get Welsa eaten. Too precocious for her own good, that girl."

Mildred felt sick.

"Your dorm is the same one we put your mother in originally." The High Witch smiled, touching a wall in front of them. It disappeared, and a door bubbled in its place. "I expect you to get along with . . . *all* the other girls in there."

Mildred nodded hesitantly.

High Witch Tractia touched the door, and it slid open.

"Go in," she said.

Mildred took a slow step through the doorway, and the door slammed behind her. She jumped. Then she caught sight of the room around her, and she shrank back.

It was huge. Thirteen beds circled the edges, with a cavernous space in the center. Twelve other girls were milling around the room, some talking, a few fighting, and one reading a book irritably. A dim chandelier flickered from the ceiling high above them, casting shadows that danced like ghosts.

"Yiella, lose those frills," one skinny girl sneered, tugging at her neighbor's bulky nightgown. "They make you look fat."

"They're supposed to," the other girl shot back. "I'm a hag."

"Hags aren't supposed to be *fat*," the skinny girl snorted. "Just ugly."

"Well, *you* aren't ugly or beautiful!"

The skinny girl gasped in outrage.

"It's a new girl!" one blonde girl squealed, pointing at the doorway. "Told you we'd get one today!"

Eleven pairs of eyes whipped to Mildred, who stepped back, unnerved. Only the black-haired girl in the back of the room didn't look up from her book.

A short, curly-haired girl hopped over to Mildred. "Who're you?" she asked. "Are you a village witch? You look like one."

"I — I —" Mildred's voice didn't seem to work right. She gulped. "I'm not. I'm from a manor. Ebony Drake."

The black-haired girl's head shot up. She stared at Mildred, eyes narrowing.

"Well, you look like a village witch," the hag said. "Boring. Like a *Normal*."

Several other girls in the room giggled.

Mildred swallowed. She wasn't going to mention her father.

"Who's your family?" the black-haired girl demanded, slamming her book shut. "What's your mother's name?"

Mildred blinked. "I — uh —" She looked around at the other girls, realizing they all wore black cloaks. She was glad Aunt Lilith had darkened her blue one. "D-Drakin."

"*My* mother's name's Lieirien," the curly-haired girl said loudly.

"She was —"

"Shut up," another girl hissed, elbowing her.

The black-haired girl's ears turned crimson. "So," she said slowly. "The High Witch put us together. It's just the sort of thing she would do."

Mildred stared at her uncertainly. "Why . . .?"

"My name's Rulisa." The girl's face had flushed as crimson as her ears. "Welsa was my mother. I'm going to be your death-enemy."

Mildred's mouth opened, stunned.

"Ooh, a blood-feud!" the curly-haired girl cried. "I've always wished I had one of those! You don't even have to *look* for enemies then!"

Mildred's stomach tightened. Her arms shook.

"W-w-we don't have to be enemies," she stammered. "Just because our mothers — I mean, I know they killed each other —"

Rulisa's eyes flashed. "*You're* the reason I have no mother," she said fiercely. "*You're* the reason I've always been laughed at. No one respects a male witch, or the daughters he raises. As soon as we've graduated, I *will* kill you."

She turned and marched back to her bed.

Mildred gaped after her.

"Wow, being *Rulisa's* enemy . . ." A short girl shivered. "Glad it's not me."

"Lucky people with blood feuds," the curly-haired girl sighed. "It's going to take me forever to find a death-enemy, I just know it."

"Hey, I do look ugly in this outfit, don't I?" the hag demanded, turning to another of the girls in the room. "Tell me I do!"

The empty bed waited between one of the hags and a blond girl named Heidanlar. Mildred took it reluctantly, wishing that Rulisa would stop shooting hostile glares in her direction.

Heidanlar wasted no time in talking to her.

"Rulisa's really powerful," she said triumphantly, "but no one likes her. Every single person in the school would love to see her crushed by an enemy. That could be you!"

"Uh . . ." Mildred said uncomfortably.

Heidanlar beamed. "In fact, since Rulisa hates you, I may even let you be friends with me. Say 'thank you'!"

"Thank . . . you . . ." Mildred said slowly.

Heidanlar giggled. "You have no idea what a privilege that can be!"

Mildred buried her head in her pillow. She didn't know, she didn't care, and just wanted to go back home.

Mildred woke up early, sweating from the nightmares she'd had about death-matches and broomsticks all night. Every muscle in her body ached, and the dim, windowless gloom didn't improve her mood.

Everyone else was still asleep. Heidanlar's golden ringlets were spread out artistically across her pillow, the rest of her body draped in pink silk. Rulisa was clad in red velvet. Both hags wore fastidiously tattered nightshirts. Mildred swallowed, looking down at herself. She looked . . . looked . . . looked drab. Neglected, even. She whispered a quick spell to smooth wrinkles from her fraying dress.

Would it have killed Aunt Oplisa to give me a nightgown? she thought resentfully.

Heidanlar yawned and stirred. She opened her eyes and looked over at Mildred.

"Oh," she murmured, looking pleased. "Most people don't get up this early. I'll show you down to breakfast if you hurry."

Mildred fastened her cloak around her shoulders slowly, then ran her fingers through her shoulder-length hair, hoping to smooth out any tangles.

Heidanlar pulled the pink silk nightgown over her head and slid on a glittering black sheathe. She snapped her fingers, and her hair sprang into perfect golden ringlets.

"Come on," she whispered, jerking her head at the doorway.

Mildred crammed her slippers on her feet and ran after her. As they passed the wyvern statue, hot air wafted across her face.

Mildred shrieked and leapt back. Not only did that thing have a pulse, it was *breathing!* What was *with* the statues in this building?

"Could you *be* more loud?" Heidanlar asked angrily.

"S-s-sorry," Mildred stammered. "I — I — I didn't mean —"

"Oh, whatever," Heidanlar sighed. "It's not like I really care if you disturb other people's sleep."

She snapped her fingers, and a solid-looking wall dissolved before them. "This way," she said.

Legs wobbling, Mildred hurried after her. They descended a spiral staircase for several minutes.

"H-Heidanlar?" she asked nervously. "H-how long do you think it'll take me to learn the school's layout? I mean, when did you memorize it?"

"Never," Heidanlar said succinctly. "Even the High Witch can't keep the school tame. Just keep a directional charm on you at all times."

Tame? Mildred wondered, staring at the walls with wide eyes. *What is this place?*

"You're the first new student we've had in weeks," Heidanlar said casually. "Usually someone graduates every week or so, but it's been slow lately. You're replacing Anaface, who was in my crowd before graduating."

"So she passed everything?" Mildred asked timidly.

"*Advanced* in everything. Passing means you take the class all over again." Heidanlar kicked a solid wall at the bottom of the staircase, waited two seconds, then pounded high above her head with her fist. "Usually it takes, oh, ten weeks in a class before you advance in things. *I* can advance in eight. Once I even did it in three."

Hurray for you, Mildred thought gloomily.

"Of course . . ." Heidanlar turned to face her, looking furious. "Rulisa's been here less than a year, and she's practically Third Class. Which is why you need to stop her. Sabotage her, maybe. At this rate, she'll graduate the same year I do, which would make her valedictorian over me. Which would *not* be okay."

Heidanlar slammed her fist into the wall, and it yawned open. She grabbed Mildred's wrist and shoved her first through the opening. Thankfully, the hallway they fell into looked more like an ordinary building, rather than a gulping throat.

Mildred breathed a sigh of relief.

"You'll probably be Fifth Class a year or so," Heidanlar went on.

"That's usually how it goes. Most people take five years to graduate. *She* — that little *know-it-all* —"

Mildred stopped to stare at a squat goblin statue, which looked scared and confused. Next to it was a sharp griffin with the fiercest claws she'd ever seen. Its eyes flashed in fury.

"— Which is why I'm so eager to see you beat her," Heidanlar finished. "Quit lingering! The breakfast hall could move at any minute."

Tearing her gaze away, Mildred ran after the older girl. She didn't want to be left alone in this building.

The breakfast hall was huge, and strewn with tables and chairs of all sizes and shapes.

Six other students were scattered across the room — three eating alone, one writing industriously, and two in a corner laughing loudly over something. The largest table, in the center, was empty.

"See what I mean?" Heidanlar yawned, waving a hand around the room. "Most people don't get up this early. I only do to make sure I get the right table. See that one in the center?"

Mildred glanced at the massive table. It looked like it could fit thirteen girls, easily. Most other tables looked sized to fit two or three.

"Do you eat with lots of people?" she asked.

Heidanlar giggled. "No, no! We're *quite* exclusive, Vaysa and me."

"Then why do you . . . ?"

"Because it shows how important we are," Heidanlar sniffed, rolling her eyes. "Honestly. Here, take a tray."

She handed a scratched, battered tray to Mildred, then hunted through the stack next to the door until she found another that looked brand new. She turned and marched towards the center table.

Mildred dragged her feet as she followed.

Heidanlar plonked her tray onto the table and said something unintelligible, wiggling her fingers over the tray. A steaming bowl of hemlock-cranberry stew appeared.

Mildred stared at her, mouth open. "How did you do that?"

Heidanlar smirked. "Old Tongue. You'll learn eventually, too. Here."

She grabbed Mildred's tray and recited the same nonsense-words over it. Another bowl of hemlock-cranberry stew appeared.

Mildred wrinkled her nose. "I hate hemlock."

Heidanlar's expression darkened. "Say 'thank you,'" she growled.

Mildred gulped. "Th-thank you."

"Ooh, look, there's Vaysa!" Heidanlar leapt up and waved wildly to someone across the room. "Hey, Vaysa! Vaaaaysa! Rulisa's just declared a death-enemy! Come meet her! We may let her eat here regularly!"

Mildred slunk down into her chair. She already hated this school.

Chapter 5

Earth, Water, Wind, and Fire

alfway through breakfast, a sheet of paper appeared beside Mildred's hand.

She jumped, knocking her spoon to the floor, which made Vaysa and Heidanlar giggle. Then she noticed they'd each received a sheet of paper too.

"Advanced Old Tongue!" Heidanlar said gleefully, picking up hers. "I advanced again. You flunked from Cauldron Cleansing to Basic Brews, though."

"I'm still one level higher than you in Elements," Vaysa retorted. She pushed aside a pair of fried death cap mushrooms to grab Heidanlar's schedule. "And you went down in Witch History."

"What are these?" Mildred asked tentatively, clutching her paper.

"Class schedules. Obviously. Let's see." Heidanlar snatched hers. She surveyed it, Vaysa peering over her shoulder. Then both burst out laughing.

"What?" Mildred asked, alarmed. "What's so funny?"

"Oh, it's just — you're in *Fundamental* Elements!"

"What's wrong with that?" Mildred cried, feeling hurt.

"It's a bottom class," Heidanlar sneered. "Though you're in third-level Traditions. That's not bad."

"Yeah," Vaysa shrugged. "But Fundamental *Elements?* How can she not know her own element already?"

Mildred shrank down in her seat. "May I please have my schedule back?"

Heidanlar smirked, leaning forward. "We can show you where your first class is, if you like."

Mildred didn't answer. She just stared at her schedule. Sighing, Heidanlar wadded it up and tossed it back.

Mildred fumbled, caught it, and folded the paper carefully in her sweaty hands.

"Of course, classes don't start until noon." Heidanlar stretched. "That's why no one bothers to wake up this early. High Witch Tractia thinks it's unhealthy to sleep before the witching hour."

"That's the hour after midnight," Vaysa added.

"I know when it is," Mildred said irritably.

"And we all get brand-new schedules today." Heidanlar yawned. "Since schedules change every week."

"Which is every thirteen days," Vaysa added.

"I *know* how long a week is!"

"So," Heidanlar said, leaning forward, "if you want to advance, just be one of the two best students in your level of a class. Then you'll go up that week."

"And make sure you're never in the bottom two," Vaysa smirked, "because then you'll go *down*."

Mildred stared at her schedule. "What happens if you fail all of the bottom classes?"

"What, all of them? Simultaneously?"

Mildred nodded.

Heidanlar rolled her eyes. "Then you get expelled. Obviously."

Mildred stared at her in horror.

"Yeah, but don't worry," Vaysa shrugged, slapping Heidanlar on the arm. "That can't happen unless you've already been here a week. New students get a grace period."

"Yeah, and you're mostly starting second-level, anyway. They must think you have a pretty solid grounding already."

Mildred's stomach clenched. *Thank you, Aunt Oplisa.* Why couldn't she have started at the bottom, just like any other brand-new student?

"There are thirteen teachers, one for every level," Vaysa added. "And they also get ranked constantly. So it's not unusual to get the same teacher for several subjects one week."

"Witch Ryaonaon," Heidanlar groused. "She's average in all subjects, so I've had weeks where she's my only teacher in *everything*."

"All Cauldron classes go first," Vaysa said, pointing at Mildred's schedule, "then Elements, Witch History, Talismans, Deadly Spells, Old Tongue, Unraveling, and Traditions. There's a different classroom for every class — one hundred and four in all — but only thirteen exist at a time. You'll learn to recognize the different doors eventually."

"I'll even help you find Cauldron Usages once we've finished eating," Heidanlar said graciously, lifting her bowl to slurp the broth remaining. "Say 'thank you.'"

"Thank you," Mildred muttered, starting to hate the words.

"There it is!" Heidanlar pointed down the hall. "Your classroom."

Mildred stared at the door. There were tiny carvings all over it, bulging cauldrons and dead animal parts. Bizarrely, it made her homesick for Aunt Hurda's disgusting cooking.

"This one's Advanced Brews." Heidanlar jabbed a thumb to indicate the door beside them. It looked like it had once had carvings, but they'd been eaten away with acid. "Sixth level of Cauldron. My class this week. These doors are usually a lot farther away."

She sounded mildly annoyed by this, as if the proximity of the lower classroom was insulting her dignity.

"Th-thank you for showing me," Mildred stammered. The sight of those doors filled her with a sense of wary revulsion. *Cauldron Usages* meant cooking. She hated cooking. On the other hand, she might learn more without Aunt Lilith and Aunt Hurda arguing about flavors every few minutes.

Heidanlar yawned. "Well? It's not locked. I recommend finding a good seat and napping until class starts. I'm going to do that in Advanced Brews."

Mildred touched the door, stomach fluttering. What if Heidanlar had sent her into the wrong classroom? What if it was even more intidimating inside than the hallway?

The Advanced Brews door slammed, and Mildred jerked back.

Now she was all alone, surrounded by a wounded tiger, three goblins, and a minotaur. All made from obsidian, all staring her direction. She had no desire to check if they were breathing.

It can't get much worse, she decided. She pushed the door gingerly, and it swung open to reveal an empty classroom.

The place was smoky and dim. Mildred blinked, rubbing her eyes, and suddenly felt exhausted. She dragged herself to the middle of the back row, shoved two flimsy-looking cauldrons out of the way, and laid her head on top of her arms.

She held the schedule out in front of her face, staring at the writing listlessly.

> **Cauldron Usages**
> **Fundamental Elements**
> **Basic Witch History**
> **Talismans and Charms**
> **Menacing Spells**
> **Old Tongue Basics**
> **Rudimentary Unraveling**
> **Intermediate Traditions**

What did those subjects mean?
Why did she have the feeling she was going to hate them all?

Lights blazed on, and the fog cleared. Mildred jerked awake.

The front two tables were full. Four girls clumped along the front row and five clustered in the middle. No one else was sitting in the back row, probably because someone had dumped the other tables' cauldrons back here.

The door opened, and a grumpy-looking hag slunk in. She muttered something under her breath and flopped into a chair on the back row. She shoved one of the piles of cauldrons off the table, where they landed with a dull *thud.* Then she flopped her head on her arm and snored loudly.

"— And your teaching style is even *more* flawed!"

Mildred froze. That voice in the hallway sounded familiar.

"Advanced theory is useless for beginners," an unfamiliar woman's voice snapped. "You had no business doing a final project on it. Which is why I flunked you last week."

"That's the most ridiculously short-sighted thing I've ever heard! If you actually tried to teach your students, High Witch Tractia might not have flunked *you* last week!"

The door slammed open, revealing the two angry faces. The ugly girl beside Mildred rubbed her eyes, looking up blearily. A grumpy expression crossed her face at sight of the teacher. She yawned, stretched, and slumped into an inattentive slouch.

"Do you seriously think students should wait until Alchemy to learn *any* theory?" Rulisa shouted. Her ears were bright red, a curl of smoke rising from each one of them. "That's one level from the top! It's absurd! I talked to Witch Hwilar last week, and she agrees!"

"You've no business talking to Witch Hwilar," the tall woman snarled. "You can't even pass Basic Brews!"

"That's because of *you,* you miserable —"

"I'm on your side, Witch Harvigna!" one of the girls from the front row cried eagerly. "You know everything! Can I do extra homework for you this week?"

Rulisa glared at her, then froze as she caught sight of Mildred.

Mildred offered a nervous smile and waved tentatively.

Rulisa stormed to the back row, grabbed one of the chairs, and shoved it at the middle table.

"Hey!" one of the crowded girls protested.

Rulisa said nothing, but two wisps of smoke trailed from the tips of both ears. Looking petulant, the other girl subsided.

Witch Harvigna stood in front of the classroom. She closed her eyes, collected herself, and slammed her fists on the front table.

"Welcome to Cauldron Usages," she snarled. "I hope we'll all share a pleasant week."

Mildred watched the words *fire, wind, water,* and *earth* cluster around the ceiling in purple smoke. She wondered what kind of spell made those.

"Welcome to Fundamental Elements," Witch Rantunla said in a monotone. "I will start by summarizing Elemental Theory."

A loud chorus of groans echoed across the room. Witch Rantunla ignored them.

"Every witch is born with a connection to earth, wind, fire, or water. This connection stays dormant until triggered, usually by danger. Once activated, the element can be used, and no longer has the capacity to harm the witch connected with it."

Bored, Mildred watched the words drifting around the ceiling.

"Sometimes witches can discover their element by accident," Witch Rantunla continued. "Usually, it takes deliberate testing."

"I know I'm not earth!" a skinny girl on Mildred's row called excitedly. "I fell out of a tree when I was eight and broke my leg!"

Witch Rantunla waved at the smoke letters above their heads. "Fire is the most powerful and hardest to control. Wind is more manageable, but has less power. Water is fairly powerful with decent control, and earth has little power, but can be controlled easily." Witch Rantunla sounded like she was reciting something. "The most powerful has the least control; the least controllable has the highest power. We call this the Elemental Continuum."

Another chorus of groans.

How could anybody possibly not know that already? Mildred thought with irritation.

"Now, some witches may believe that power means everything," Witch Rantunla went on. "This is a fallacy. An earth witch could do far more damage with magical poison than a fire witch could with open flame — given the right circumstances."

The pudgy girl beside Mildred snickered.

"Is something funny, Laynan?" Witch Rantunla demanded.

"Well, yeah. Given the right circumstances, a *Normal* could beat a fire witch, but — come on. In a direct showdown, power's going to win. Who cares if you can't control it and you get some collateral damage? Big deal. It's not like it's going to hurt you. And who wouldn't take immunity to heat over a few extra edible poisons?"

A rumble of agreement spread across the class.

Witch Rantunla looked irritated. "That is not the only —"

"Besides, why are most of the teachers here fire or wind?" Laynan cut in. "Why is our High Witch always fire? Why is Kraken Institute a joke, while Smoldering is our greatest enemy?"

Another rumble of assent.

"We've had talented instructors here with earth or water magic before," Witch Rantunla snapped. "Fyrailn, who's teaching Elemental Command this week —"

Which level is that? Mildred wondered.

"— also Witch Ryaonaon, not to mention Oplisa, the infamous valedictorian —"

Mildred's head jerked up. *Aunt Oplisa was a valedictorian?*

"Oplisa!" a voice in the back spat. Mildred spun around to see an older girl who looked furious. "She's no example. She kills witches as often as Normals. It's a *disgrace*."

Several other girls around the classroom nodded and murmured. One snarled something about her brother. Another muttered about a grandfather.

Mildred slunk down in her chair. *Oh, good. More prospective enemies.*

Witch Rantunla sighed. "Be that as it may, she is a powerful water witch. On to elemental testing. Stand up!"

The girls in the back groaned.

"Do we have to do this every week?" a girl behind Mildred whined. "You've tested me for four weeks running."

"If you wish to avoid going through it next week, you'll try harder to advance to Basic Elements now, won't you?" Witch Rantunla snapped. "Stand up!"

In a mass of grumbles, the girls assembled into a long line. Mildred let the others elbow her to the back.

"You." Witch Rantunla pointed at the skinny girl at the front of the line. She'd been in the front row with Mildred.

"Me?" the girl squeaked.

"This is your first time being tested, isn't it?"

Shaking, the girl nodded.

"Name?" Witch Rantunla demanded.

"H-Haglin."

"Fine." The instructor pulled a sack from a pocket on the inside of her cloak. She held it over Haglin's head.

"You're not going to muss my hair, are you?" the skinny girl asked nervously.

Witch Rantunla smirked. The sack opened, dumping a mountain of dirt down on her. A muffled shriek came from inside it. "I canh't breafthe!"

Several of the girls in the line snickered.

The instructor waved her hand, and the dirt sucked itself back into the sack.

Haglin looked at her dirty hands and started to sob. "I'm filthy!"

Witch Rantunla's smirk widened. "We can fix that."

Haglin's eyes widened in horror. "Oh — no —!"

Witch Rantunla opened a second sack, and a jet of water slammed Haglin against the wall. Her screams dissolved in bubbles until the teacher closed it again.

"I'm so-o-oaaaaaked," she wailed, collapsing on the ground and sobbing.

Witch Rantunla ignored this. "Next."

Haglin froze from trying to wring her dress out. "Next?"

Witch Rantunla twisted a third sack from her robes.

Once again, Haglin slammed into the classroom wall. She shrieked about her hair getting tangled. Then her eyes bulged. She fell to the ground, gasping and clutching her throat.

Witch Rantunla closed the third sack. "Suffocation. Not wind either."

She summoned a huge fireball in her hand.

Haglin screamed and ducked. The fireball dove straight after her, blazed around her clothing — and then fizzled, vanishing in a puff of smoke.

Haglin clung to the sleeves of her dress, which were drenched and torn and dirty, but without a single scorch mark on them.

"I'm fire?" she whimpered.

"Apparently." Witch Rantunla grabbed her arm and shoved her to the side of the room. "Sit down. Next!"

The second girl, Danyarsa, didn't seem to mind the mountain of dirt dumped on her head. Nor did she look surprised when the water vanished before it hit her.

"Water," Witch Rantunla announced. "Next!"

Gyrinal was wind — her clothes didn't even move as Witch Rantunla opened the sack, even though the girl behind her lost her schedule and had to run after it.

Keenlin was fire.

Ainlar was fire.

Suzarx was earth.

Trasia was wind.

Laynan was fire.

"Obviously," the pudgy girl grumbled as she headed to the other side of the room. "I've already been tested."

Arzsanya was water.

Fiora was fire.

Killyan was earth.

Raginreln was fire.

Mildred looked around. She was the only person left.

"Name?" Witch Rantunla demanded.

Mildred swallowed. "M-Mildred."

Witch Rantunla released the mountain of dirt.

Mildred gaped in sudden darkness. Then she realized that it was growing tighter. Crushing, crushing, crushing . . .

"Get it off!" she screamed, panicking.

The dirt vanished.

"Not earth," Witch Rantunla noted. She opened the sloshing sack.

The jet of water slammed her against the wall. Mildred tried to draw in a breath, inhaled water, and choked. She fell to the ground, coughing desperately.

Relieved that Witch Rantunla had given her time to recover, she stumbled to her feet, rubbed her eyes, opened them, and started to ask, "When —"

The third sack was open.

"Plenty of power," Witch Rantunla muttered, closing the third sack. "Little control. You'll be worse than most fire witches."

Mildred's mouth gaped open. "I'm . . . wind?"

"Obviously. Sit down."

Mildred scrambled for her seat.

I'm wind, she thought, astonished. She realized she'd expected to be earth, or water. But . . . wind . . .

A slow smile crept across her face. *Wind!* The one element none of her aunts had, and it was *hers!* She was different! She was separate! She was unique!

Mildred stopped, her jubilation fizzling.

Drakin was wind.

She had the same element as her mother.

Chapter 6

Witch History

Opening the door of Basic Witch History, Mildred smiled in triumph. She'd found the classroom all on her own!

. . . And there was Rulisa.

Not another class with her, Mildred thought, dismayed. *Shouldn't she be in higher levels than me?*

"A new sstudent, I ssee," a ragged voice hissed.

Mildred glanced at the front of the room and blanched. Their teacher was apparently a hideous old woman with matted hair and a complexion to match. Every drawn-out sibilance she spoke shot spray in the air. Mildred had never thought she would meet anybody uglier than Aunt Hurda, but this woman had managed it.

"In thiss classsroom," the hag hissed, "one asskss newesst sstudentss ssit with the oldesst. It promotess cooperation."

Mildred glanced at the open seat in the middle of the front row. Both older girls on each side looked eager to pick on their new classmate. She wondered how the teacher had drawn that conclusion.

"One beginss one'ss firsst lessson of thiss week," the hag announced, scratching her arms with grimy fingernails, "with each sstudent reciting family hisstory. Time iss not limited. Pleasse fill one'ss whole classs period. Sstudentss may fill tomorrow'ss classs alsso, if needed."

Mildred peeked at the back two rows. Two students behind her were yawning, three looked glassy-eyed, and one was napping.

This does not bode well, she decided.

The classroom door slammed open. Mildred jumped. A tall witch stood in the hall, emanating fury.

"Witch Hoiyanar," she snapped. Her eyes flashed. "High Witch Tractia wishes to see you."

"Fyrailn!" The hag looked alarmed. "Er . . . one wonderss about a reasson?"

The tall witch's mouth twisted. "We're switching schedules this week."

The hag's eyes widened. "*Sswitching? Uss?* Don't you alwayss teach the thirteenth-level classsess?"

"Yes, Hoiyanar," Witch Fyrailn said tightly. "So why don't you get going."

"But one doess not undersstand." Witch Hoiyanar looked baffled. "What did one do to earn thiss?"

"*You* did not do anything," Witch Fyrailn snarled. "*I* did not do anything. It's Ryaonaon's doing."

"Ryaonaon?" The hideous teacher looked even more confused. "But one thinkss that sshe defected —"

"— to Kraken Institute this morning, yes, yes." Witch Fyrailn looked impatient. "Leaving us one teacher short with no notice. Meaning that the High Witch needed to substitute this week. Meaning she just *had* to take all the highest-level classes."

The light seemed to dawn for Witch Hoiyanar. "One ssusspectss you objected to thiss?"

Witch Fyrailn looked surly. "She said if I was going to complain, I could switch my schedule this week with the lowest teacher's."

Witch Hoiyanar clapped her hands with glee. "One iss mosst pleassed!"

"Just go!" Witch Fyrailn muttered, jabbing her finger at the door. "A room full of intelligent, well-behaved First Class students is awaiting your instruction."

"Well, one doess what one musst!" The hag seized a pile of papers from the desk in front of the room. Several spilled on the floor, but she didn't seem to notice. She fled the room, cackling.

There was a long silence after the hag left. Witch Fyrailn appeared to be attempting to control her fury.

"All right," she said finally, her voice low. "I am not accustomed to teaching Fifth Class students, but it seems I have little choice. So I will start by saying —"

She stopped abruptly, her eyes on Rulisa.

One of the older girls in the back stood up.

"Um, Witch Fyrailn?" she said nervously. "We were just about to recite personal histories when you —"

Witch Fyrailn shook herself. "Fine. Go ahead. Start things."

The older girl ran her fingers through her black hair, looking nervous and excited. She seemed eager to impress their new teacher. "I'm the daughter of Optura. She graduated here in less than four years, and she was one of the finest scholars this school has ever seen. Her element was fire, like mine. My father is Foyralian. Both my grandmothers and all four of great-grandmothers attended Black Magic Academy, as have all my female ancestors for the past six —"

Witch Fyrailn looked bored. "Next."

Looking scared, another girl stood up. "W-Witch Fyrailn," she said. "May I just say what an honor —"

"No," Witch Fyrailn snapped. "Get on with your history."

The student gulped. "I — my mother graduated from here. She was named Lyonka. Um . . . my father, Yoniklan, didn't get into any school." Several giggles echoed around the room. "Both had fire as their element," she added quickly, flushing as she sat down.

Witch Fyrailn stifled a yawn. "Next."

Rulisa stood up slowly. "My mother's name was Welsa. She was salutatorian the year she graduated from this school. *Would* have been valedictorian, in fact, had her death-enemy not sabotaged —"

"Stick with the facts," Witch Fyrailn snapped. "Let's avoid wild speculation."

Rulisa's eyes flashed. "Fine. My father is Horinwa, valedictorian of Kraken Institute. His mother, Kanostra, was High Witch of the Sukinal School of Magical Studies for thirty-four years. I intend to graduate in less than half the usual time. You should see me in your thirteenth-level classes next year."

Witch Fyrailn's eyes narrowed. "You have your mother's arrogance, I see. Next."

The curly-haired girl from Mildred's dorm bounced to her feet.

"My mother's name is Lieirien," she said eagerly, "and my father's name is Karkan. Just wait until you hear which awards they've won!"

"Good idea," Witch Fyrailn snapped. "Next."

Looking crushed, the girl slumped into her seat.

Mildred cringed back further as Witch Fyrailn's finger whipped around the room. Each history seemed to outdo all the ones before it. Were people lying? Could there *really* be this many valedictorians and scholars in every family? Was she supposed to know how to brag shamelessly like this?

"Next." Witch Fyrailn pointed at her.

Mildred stumbled to her feet.

"I — I — I'm named Mildred," she gulped. "My mother's name was Drakin. She was valedictorian here. And — I — um — that's it."

"Drakin's daughter?" For the first time, Witch Fyrailn looked interested. "Are you really?"

Mildred swallowed. "Y-yes . . . ?"

Witch Fyrailn smiled. For the first time, the scorn disappeared from her eyes. "We were such friends in school! But we lost touch after she got married. And then she died, of course. How are Lilith and Anklistine?"

Mildred stared at her, astonished. "You . . . know my aunts?"

"Oh, yes. I quite liked Anklistine. Hated Oplisa. Didn't know Lilith well. Hurda was a weird one. Which did you grow up with?"

"Um . . . all of them," Mildred said nervously. "In the family manor. Ebony Drake."

"Ah. Then Oplisa won." Witch Fyrailn frowned. "Pity. Drakin didn't want that curse put on them."

"Curse?" Mildred asked, startled.

"The one to stop their younger sisters leaving home without permission." Witch Fyrailn looked at her curiously. "Did you never notice it was present?"

Mildred swallowed. She knew all three of the younger aunts complained bitterly about their oldest sister when she wasn't around. Of course they wouldn't live with her, if they'd been given a choice.

"Drakin had such loftier plans," Witch Fyrailn said wistfully. "New power-bases in each city, every kingdom. Marrying her sisters to the most powerful witches of Guraton, thus refreshing several bloodlines. Ruling all Four Kingdoms behind the scenes . . ."

Mildred shuddered. This did not sound like an improvement.

"Oplisa was a short-sighted *fool*," Witch Fyrailn spat, "forcing everyone to keep their powers 'pure' and 'concentrated.' All she did was prevent future generations of her own family."

Mildred picked at the peeling wood tabletop. She knew Aunt Anklistine had been engaged, back when she was little — and Aunt Oplisa had killed her sweetheart, just to stop her sister leaving. Aunt Anklistine had more reason than anyone to hate her older sister, and sometimes it showed on her face.

It would have been nice to have cousins, Mildred thought sadly.

"Of course," Witch Fyrailn said slyly, "'short-sighted foolishness' leads right to the beginning of our lesson. And so . . ."

She pulled a burr from her robe, tossed it at the floor, and a bush exploded through the obsidian. Thorny purple berries burst out all over it.

"We are going to learn to not lie to our teachers today," she said pleasantly.

The curly-haired girl from Mildred's dorm leapt backwards, her chair clattering off to the side. "What is that thing?!"

"Truth poison." Witch Fyrailn smiled and squeezed a berry, which sizzled venomously. "Only earth witches are immune to it. Shall we hear those family histories all over again?"

Feeling dazed from the fumes, but significantly less sick than the bragging students had been, Mildred stumbled out into the hallway.

"Having fun?" Rulisa asked acidly.

Mildred yelped and tripped over a spiked tail. She landed *splat* onto a statue.

"I'm sure you think you're so amazing," Rulisa spat. "Your mother was best friends with the most influential teacher in school. Well, I have news for you: Witch Fyrailn does *not* rank students based on personal preference. She is ruthless in her pursuit of accuracy. You will *not* be getting free advancements this week."

Mildred winced and pulled herself off the feathered lizard. She was glad it hadn't been one of the monsters with quills.

"Rulisa," she said, frustrated, rubbing a sharp bruise on her leg, "why must you always assume the worst about me? I don't care who ranks highest. I'm not after free advancement."

"Oh, cut the false modesty." Rulisa looked disgusted. "I hate pretenders."

"I'm not pretending!" Mildred cried. "I don't even want to be death-enemies!"

"Oh, of *course* you don't," Rulisa sneered. "Like you're really going to ignore the entire reason you were born."

Mildred stared at her. "What?" she asked, baffled.

"Drakin never planned to have children with Thurgold!" Rulisa snarled. "Not until my mother had me! Then Drakin immediately decided to get pregnant — to give Welsa's child a death-enemy!"

"That's *not* the reason!" Mildred shouted. "I was just a mistake!"

"That's not what she told Welsa! She *said* that you were born to kill me! That's why they held the death-match in the first place!"

Mildred fell silent. Unfortunately, that seemed entirely likely. Knowing Drakin —

Something else Rulisa had said penetrated.

"... Thurgold?" she said slowly. "Was that ... my father's name?"

"Oh, don't pretend you don't know," Rulisa said disgustedly.

Mildred reached out to steady her arm on a statue. Then, feeling a throbbing pulse, she hastily jerked her hand away.

"Who was he?" she asked quietly, her voice shaking. "Why did she choose him? And is he — is my father — still alive?"

Rulisa stared at her. "You actually don't know?"

Mildred shook her head, trembling.

Rulisa was silent a long moment.

"Nobody to us," she said finally. "But yes, he is still alive. If you ever feel like lowering yourself to talk to Normals, I'm sure you could find him someplace."

Mildred was surprised to find Vaysa in Talismans and Charms beside her.

"I thought you were Third Class!" she whispered, sitting next to her in the middle row. "Shouldn't you be in a higher level?"

Vaysa made a face. "I hate this class. I keep flunking down. Don't worry, I'll advance back again next week."

"Yanfarell, pass around these textbooks," Witch Dhadia ordered, pointing to a pile of thick books teetering on her desk. "Then everyone turn to the introduction, where you will read that — Uplanda, illusions are to be worn *after* class — talismans are power-storing objects that are, strongest to weakest: talismans, amulets, baubles, and charms. Yorkfa, why are you not following along?"

Mildred flipped to the introduction, then stared at the words in dismay. Like all books, it was handwritten — but unlike most, the author seemed to have never studied penmanship. She glanced over at Vaysa's copy, but the writing was no closer to legible.

"I hate this textbook," Vaysa muttered. "You'd think, after a century, they'd bother to find someone different to copy it over."

"This week," Witch Dhadia went on, "you will learn how to create five simple charms, as well as memorizing power differentials between talisman types. There are charts to help you with this . . ."

Mildred turned the page to find a chart of unintelligible numbers that continued for the next seventy pages. The few paragraphs of explanation were entirely in Old Tongue, and half of those even looked smudged. She stared at it in horror.

"Like I said," Vaysa muttered, "I hate this class."

Menacing Spells was unpleasant. Old Tongue Basics wasn't terrible, but Mildred felt lost without fundamentals to build upon. Rudimentary Unraveling proved to be easily the most boring thing she had ever studied.

Intermediate Traditions, her last class of the day, was downright obnoxious.

"Why do we have to have Traditions *as well as* Witch History?" Mildred complained to Heidanlar as they headed towards the dinner hall. "They're basically the same thing, aren't they?"

"Of course they're not," Heidanlar said airily. "History's about the *past*. Traditions are about the *future*."

Mildred opened her mouth to retort — *That's completely ridiculous!* — when she was distracted by the sight of Vaysa tossing paper in the air and grinning. A short, plain girl was jumping up and trying to grab it from her.

"What's Vaysa doing?" Mildred asked, alarmed.

"Huh?" Heidanlar barely glanced backwards. "Oh, just bullying Trasia. She's pathetic. Ignore her."

Trasia blasted the paper out of Vaysa's hands, grabbed it from the air, and stormed off.

"That didn't seem pathetic to me," Mildred said.

Heidanlar snorted. "Believe me, she's a social pariah. And with many good reasons. So don't ever speak to her. Just ignore her."

Mildred stared at her indignantly. *Since when do you decide who I speak to?*

"That was hilarious!" Vaysa chortled, jogging over to them. "Who wants dinner?"

"Tell you what," Heidanlar said, putting her arm around Mildred. "Let's go down to the dinner hall. I'll even let you pick your own food. Won't that make you happy?"

Mildred clutched the badge on her chest. *No,* she thought with irritation. *That will not make me happy, you arrogant . . .*

A moment later, she was fighting to get the badge out of her hair again.

Chapter 7
Village Witch

By the end of Mildred's first week at the Academy, she was exhausted. Her workload was tremendous, and she had no idea what she was doing in any classes except Witch History. Worse, she suspected that Witch Fyrailn was the only teacher with a good opinion of her.

That suspicion was confirmed on the first day of her second week, when their new schedules appeared over breakfast. Heidanlar and Vaysa snatched Mildred's before she could see it. Then both burst out laughing.

"What?" Mildred asked nervously. "What's wrong?"

"You — you went down in almost every single class!" Heidanlar howled, holding up the paper with shaking hands. "That's pathetic!"

Mildred grabbed the paper from her, horrified and certain that Heidanlar had exaggerated. But she hadn't. Her schedule now read:

>   Cauldron Fundamentals
>   Fundamental Elements
>   Intermediate Witch History
>   Fundamental Talismans
>   Disagreeable Spells
>   Old Tongue Fundamentals
>   Fundamental Unraveling

"I went down in every class except Witch History!" she wailed, feeling close to tears.

Vaysa brandished her new schedule with a smirk. "I advanced a class," she bragged. "And failed nothing."

Heidanlar seized the schedule and let out a cry of dismay. "You advanced in *two* classes! Basic Talismans *and* Advanced Traditions!"

"Oh, really?" Vaysa asked innocently. "I hadn't noticed. I guess my advancing is so common that the detail just escaped me. Your schedule's unchanged this week, isn't it?"

"I'll advance three classes next week, just wait," Heidanlar muttered.

Mildred clutched her schedule, lump in her throat. She'd been working as hard as she could — it didn't seem fair to fail everything anyway. Sure, Talismans and Charms and Old Tongue Basics, but why all the rest? Had she really been *that* bad a student?

"You're going to have to shape up," Heidanlar said sternly, tapping Mildred's schedule with her long fingernails. "I mean, even if you're brand new, we can't be seen with a student in all bottom classes."

"I never *asked* to be seen with you!" Mildred exploded. She leapt to her feet. "I don't even *like* you!"

Heidanlar drew back, looking angry. "Careful."

"Apologize," Vaysa ordered.

Mildred hesitated. Then she saw the glint of malice in Vaysa's eyes.

"*NO!*" Mildred shouted. She snatched her schedule off the table and ran out of the room.

It wasn't until she was halfway down the hallway that she realized that, not only did she not know where to find her first classroom, she had no idea which way their dorm was likely to be.

Mildred wandered down the hallway, her stomach twisting. There was no way she was going back to Heidanlar or Vaysa now, but she didn't want to be late to Cauldron Fundamentals, either. Even it if wasn't due to start for awhile, if she didn't know where to find it . . .

She grabbed her schedule from her pocket, crumpled it up in a ball, and threw it at the wall.

I HATE this Academy! she thought furiously. *Why can't I find even one friend here? I wish I had ONE!*

A door near her slammed open, and the plain girl she'd seen last week stormed out.

She crumpled up a piece of paper and hurled it against the wall. It bounced, landed on Mildred's paper, and both rolled across the floor.

There was silence as they both stared at them. Mildred felt her face heat up with embarrassment.

The plain girl started to snort with laughter. She walked over, picked up the balls of paper, and handed one over.

"All bottom classes too, huh?" she asked wryly.

Mildred took the schedule and smoothed it out, face still hot with embarrassment. "Actually . . . two of them are higher," she admitted. "And I even advanced in one. Just went down in everything else."

"Oh, boo hoo," the plain girl snorted. "Try being here for two years and still getting stuck in bottom classes. Then you'll have a reason to throw out your schedule."

"Two years?" Mildred repeated, stunned. "Two *years?*"

"Yep," the girl said. "Because I'm a village witch. No one gives me a fair shot to do anything."

Village witch . . .

Mildred drew back. She'd heard the term before. They were inferior. Weak. Barely one step above Normals.

On the other hand, that sounded like something Heidanlar would say.

The plain girl was watching her.

Mildred drew in a breath. "Vaysa's a brute," she said at last. "Heidanlar's worse. If I have to hang around them any longer, I'll probably kill them. And then I'd get expelled for sure. As far as I'm concerned, they're the ones who are inferior."

A burst of laughter escaped the other girl.

"I'm social suicide," she said. "I'm sure they've told you that, and it's true. Really."

"Why?" Mildred asked hotly. "Because you're actually nice?"

"Nah, because I'm lower-class. And my class load's embarrassing. And I may have sassed Heidanlar repeatedly."

Mildred's eyes widened. She started laughing.

"Yeah," the girl grinned. "It's satisfying."

"I'm Mildred," Mildred said.

"Trasia." The girl cocked her head to the side. "I'm heading down to breakfast right now. Want to humiliate yourself and join me?"

Heidanlar started to smirk as Mildred headed back in. Then, as Trasia followed at her elbow, her eyes widened in rage.

Just ignore them, Mildred told herself, heart pounding. She fumbled for the top tray. *Just ignore them . . .*

"Oh, not that one." Trasia snatched the tray away from her. "It's badly cracked. The food would taste horrible."

Mildred stared at her. "Really?"

Trasia nodded. "Of course. All spells are better fresh. Pick one that looks newer."

No wonder Heidanlar and Vaysa always kept the best trays, Mildred thought with annoyance, searching through the stack beside Trasia.

"Here's a good one!" Trasia held up a moderately-cracked tray. "Want it?"

"Oh. Sure," Mildred said, surprised.

Trasia found another that looked slightly better and pointed to a tiny corner table at the back of the room. "Okay with you?"

Mildred nodded.

"Two walls keep people from sneaking up on me," Trasia explained as they headed across the center of room. Mildred flushed and ducked her head as they passed Heidanlar and Vaysa. "How well do you speak Old Tongue, by the way?"

"Old Tongue?" Mildred repeated, taking a seat at the tiny table across from Trasia. It was barely big enough to fit two sets of knees underneath. "I just flunked down to Fundamentals."

"Figures," Trasia said glumly. "I was hoping that was the class you'd advanced in. I don't suppose you know how to say 'dragon shrimp'?"

Mildred scrunched her face up, thinking. "I think *drakon* means 'dragon' — that's the root of my mother's name —"

"Which still doesn't give me 'shrimp,'" Trasia sighed. "Oh, well.

Turnip porridge again."

She raised the tray over her head and *cracked* it down against the table. A bowl of steaming mush appeared with a dented spoon beside it.

"Won't that break the tray?" Mildred asked uncertainly.

"Of course, eventually. It gets worse every time someone does this." Trasia eyed the lumpy porridge with distaste. "The High Witch thinks it's funny to make us break our own trays."

"I don't like her sense of humor," Mildred muttered.

"And I don't like *her*." Trasia forced a spoonful of mashed turnip and oats into her mouth. "I hate that I was named after the High Witch."

Mildred blinked. "You were?"

"Of course I was. Trasia, Tractia — same Old Tongue root: *traekah*, which means 'power.' My great-aunt suggested it. I have no idea why my parents agreed."

Mildred watched Trasia force another spoon of turnip mush into her mouth, holding her nose. Mildred's stomach growled.

"Um . . . how do you make porridge, again . . .?"

"Oh, I can do that for you." Trasia reached across the table and grabbed Mildred's tray. She brought it down against the table with a hard *thwack*, and another bowl of porridge appeared. This time, the bowl looked cracked and the spoon warped.

Mildred hesitantly dug in. It tasted worse than it looked.

"This reminds me of Mom's cooking," Trasia grumbled. "She's great at farming but has no sense of which ingredients go together. Your parents any better?"

"My mother's dead," Mildred admitted. "My father . . ."

She hesitated. Should she mention that he was a Normal? Should she ask if Trasia knew his name?

"He raised you *alone?*" Trasia asked, horrified.

"No," Mildred snapped. "I was raised by my aunts. I've never even met him."

"Oh." Trasia looked relieved. "So how did she die? Your mom?"

"Death-match," Mildred admitted. "With her death-enemy."

"Ooh!" Trasia's face lit up. "Are you going to avenge her?"

Mildred blinked. "What?"

"Blood-feud," Trasia explained eagerly.

"That sounds like what Rulisa told me," Mildred muttered.

"Ru . . . lisa?" Trasia repeated slowly. "Why were you talking with her?"

"Because she's my death-enemy."

Trasia went pale. "Ugh. I wouldn't want a blood feud with *Rulisa.*"

"Me neither." Mildred slumped against the table. "I'm starting to think she's the most powerful witch in school."

"She is," Trasia said. "It was nice knowing you."

Mildred glared. "You are not helping."

"I was not trying to." Trasia grinned. "But come on, it was a little bit funny, wasn't it?"

Chapter 8
The Witching Hour

Lights blazed in the middle of the room.

"Downstairs!" High Witch Tractia's voice boomed. "It's the witching hour of the new moon! Everyone outside!"

Mildred opened her eyes blearily. The witching hour? She'd just barely gone to sleep. Why were they supposed to wake up now?

She rubbed her eyes and noticed that the dorm was mostly empty. Three girls seemed to be stirring under their sheets, while another was hastily dressing in frills. Rulisa marked her place in a book, setting it aside.

Heidanlar sat bolt upright. "It's feeding time!" she shrieked. "I almost *forgot!*"

Mildred pulled her cloak out from under her bed, shoved on her slippers, and yanked the badge out of her hair — again. Gyrinal left the same time she did.

"What's this all about?" Mildred whispered, as they hurried through the hallway. "Is it important?"

"Yah, it's new moon," Gyrinal said blearily.

"But what does that —"

"It's *new moon,*" Gyrinal mumbled, as if she were an idiot.

The crowd squeezed through the hallways and out the front doors of the Academy, which yawned like a mouthful of teeth.

"Welcome!" High Witch Tractia boomed to the crowd massing outside. Trees that had been here before seemed to have drawn away, leaving a huge, gaping clearing. "Everyone here? One hundred and sixty-nine students and thirteen teachers?"

From the entrance, Witch Andracsa waved a hand and nodded. Their newest teacher, Witch Kanblair, clapped her hands and looked excited.

"Tartloe!" the High Witch bellowed. "It's your turn to select an honor student! Whom do you choose?"

An ancient-looking woman pointed to a tall student beside her. "Eidla."

"Eidla!" High Witch Tractia looked pleased. "Very well. First Class student Eidla has been chosen by Witch Tartloe to receive the honor. Step forward!"

The tall, dark-skinned girl pushed through the crowd to reach the High Witch. She looked smug and slightly nervous.

"Set the wards," the High Witch ordered.

Eidla held out her hands and murmured under her breath. A wall of water exploded all around them, encircling the clearing in a reflective barrier.

High Witch Tractia touched the surface near her. After a moment, she withdrew her hand. "Adequate. This will hold. Begin."

Eidla closed her eyes and held her arms far over her head. She chanted for a moment, her voice growing steadily louder. Then, with a fierce thrust, she yanked her hands at the wards and jerked a screaming creature through.

Mildred gaped and stumbled back.

"Yes!" an older girl near her shouted. "Get it, Eidla!"

Blue fire blazed and red water flashed. The black unicorn reared, horn glinting silver, and lunged to spear Eidla. She lashed it with a water-whip and drove it back towards the Academy.

"A karkadann," Gyrinal whispered, sounding awestruck. "I never knew they existed."

"Oh, they exist," the older student near them murmured. "I've seen one before, but it was purple-flamed. Eidla must have summoned this one all the way from the Kokavi Desert."

The creature's flame-tail lashed Eidla's cheek. She flinched, tightened her grip on the water-whip, and flung it at the creature, driving it back —

Driving it —

Mildred's eyes widened. That entrance *was* a mouthful of teeth!

The karkadann screamed, and a pair of glowing red eyes opened. Teeth slammed shut and the whole building rumbled, stirring.

High Witch Tractia bellowed something in Old Tongue. The building's eyes turned dark again and closed. Slowly, the entrance opened, revealing a karkadann frozen rearing, screaming at the ceiling.

Our school is a stone-turned dragon?!

"All right, back inside," High Witch Tractia said, brushing her hands. "We'll be safe until the moon's dark again. Eidla, you advance to Elemental Command this week."

"Thank you, High Witch," the dark-skinned girl beamed.

No wonder killing's forbidden on Academy grounds, Mildred thought numbly. *If that monster ever gets a taste for human flesh, we're done for.*

"Congratulations," Witch Granwir snapped, tossing Mildred her homework assignment. "Highest percentage in the class. Now, if you'd just pay attention to your practical work, you might actually advance next week."

Mildred picked up the assignment, her face flushing with pride. She wasn't fond of Unraveling, but at least the homework seemed easy. Which was a good thing, given how little sleep she'd gotten after the witching hour last night.

"— for those of you who have been begging for extra credit, *Tyra*, you may complete a project on different types of Breakers for me by tomorrow. I've spoken with Witch Taelantri, and she says you may make this a joint assignment for Advanced Traditions, as well."

Two girls in the middle row cheered.

"*But!*" Witch Granwir cleared her throat meaningfully. "*But!* If that's what you mean to do, you'll have to research *traditional* Breakers, and it will have to be very thorough indeed. And don't even think about working together. Yorkfa?"

The older girl looked nervous. "Um, are Breakers those Normals you kill to break curses, or those ones you tie to someone else's life to injure them, or . . .?"

"This is why you never advance," Witch Granwir snarled. "Given that this is Unraveling and not Deadly Spells, which one seems more likely?"

"Have you ever heard of Breakers?" Mildred whispered.

"Nope," Trasia shrugged.

"Maybe we should try the extra work, too!" Mildred whispered, excited. "We could advance this week!"

"You try," Trasia said, snorting. "It's a waste of my effort."

"Hush up, back there!" Witch Granwir shouted. "At least look like you're paying attention!"

Chapter 9
Familiar Talismans

alking into Fundamental Talismans, Mildred realized that three of their classmates were missing.

Worse, Witch Harvigna, who had been in a bad mood ever since the High Witch had demoted her to this class, had a wicked glint in her eyes.

This didn't bode particularly well.

"Good morning, girls!" Witch Harvigna crowed. "We'll be joined by several students from higher classes soon. Trasia, we don't need you today."

Trasia blinked, looking surprised. "Oh! We're doing that again, already?"

"Every thirteenth week like always, of course. Why don't you join Talismans and Charms for today?"

Trasia shot a quick glance over at Mildred. "Actually, I'd rather stay here. See what everyone gets."

Witch Harvigna shrugged. "Suit yourself. You wouldn't learn much in one day, anyway."

The door slammed open, and Rulisa stormed in. "You wanted to see me, Witch Harvigna?"

Their teacher positively smirked. "Why, yes, Rulisa, come in. Did Witch Rantunla explain why you've been sent to my classroom?"

"No," Rulisa muttered, folding her arms.

"Well, sit down, and I'll explain — ah, here's our last girl!"

A shy-looking girl who was, Mildred thought, named Killyan

poked her head through the open doorway. "I-is this where Witch Granwir asked me to come?" she asked in a small voice.

"Indeed." Witch Harvigna's eyes glinted again. "Now that everyone's here, I will explain why our class composition is different today. Each of you has entered the Academy in the last thirteen weeks. Which means that today —"

"OH!" Gyrinal gasped. "Familiar talismans!"

Rulisa stiffened.

Mildred stared at their teacher. She thought she'd heard the term before, but didn't know what it meant.

"Silence!" Witch Harvigna barked. The murmuring trickled off. "Now, let me explain the history of this tradition —"

"Witch Harvigna?" Rulisa interrupted in a haughty voice. "I don't need a familiar, and I shouldn't be here with all these beginners. If you'll just excuse me —"

"SILENCE!" Witch Harvigna snarled. "Do you want me to take this to the High Witch?"

Rulisa's ears turned crimson.

"Now," Witch Harvigna continued, "I will tell you this event's history."

Interested, Mildred leaned forward.

"Many centuries ago, the ancient center of the Forest Beyond had the power to read hearts and reveal secrets. After several Normals used it to discover the location of Black Magic Academy, High Witch Edglantia decided this had to change."

Everyone else was nodding. Mildred glanced back at Rulisa, who was staring forward with clenched teeth.

"But this power was not so simple to conquer. Every time she destroyed the place, it reformed elsewhere. So, at last, she came up with a plan to tame it."

"And turn it into the Familiar Grove!" Haglin squealed.

Witch Harvigna shot her a look of irritation. "And turn it into the Familiar Grove. This place is now used by every student, to receive a talisman that symbolizes their inner nature."

"Have you gone already?" Mildred whispered to her friend, feeling a tingle of anticipation.

"Roc," Trasia said. She pulled down the front of her dress, revealing a tiny gold disc dangling on a silver chain. There was a bird imprinted on it. "Nothing spectacular, but it suits me."

"Later, when you reach Second or First Class," Witch Harvigna went on loudly, over the top of everyone's talking, "there will be a class to show you how to use these to best effect. Because they are links to your minds, they will help you focus and control your magic. Some even grant extra power later, when you've learned how to use them properly."

"Mom has a cerberus," Trasia whispered. "She says it was worth the fifteen years to graduate, just getting that. She can talk to dogs with it."

"*Only* our Academy has this tradition," Witch Harvigna continued proudly. "No other school claims access to such a unique power. Every student who graduates takes her familiar with her. They are far more valuable for beginners, but they have some . . . uses for experienced witches, too."

THAT's where I've heard the term! Mildred realized. *Aunt Anklistine wears hers occasionally!*

Witch Harvigna stood, moving towards the doorway. She gestured for them to follow her. Chairs scraped and slippers thundered as the classroom obeyed.

"Family members have requested the right to watch," Witch Harvigna announced as they headed down the hallway. Mildred noticed a crowd gathering. Older students kept sneaking out of their classrooms to join them. "As is customary, they have been permitted. Killyan?"

The shy girl swallowed and pointed behind them. "U-um . . . are the older students allowed to follow us?"

"It's permitted," Witch Harvigna shrugged. "They can make up their work later."

Killyan's shoulders slumped.

"That's her sister," Trasia whispered, pointing. "They're in my dorm together. Killyan hates it."

The entrance's gaping maw didn't seem nearly as terrifying by day, but Mildred still flinched as they ducked under the teeth. Trasia said she'd been through three new moons now, since she'd been here for almost two years, but Mildred would never — *ever* — get used to it.

"Mama!" Haglin squealed, pushing past Mildred. "Uncle!"

Witch Harvigna waited by the entrance and counted them as they exited. Rulisa stomped out last, her ears smoldering.

"You'll never believe what I've learned so far!" Laynan babbled to her two fat parents. "I'm in third-level Old Tongue, and I'm up to Frightening Spells already . . ."

"Mildred!"

Mildred's eyes widened. She knew that voice.

"Mildred!" Aunt Lilith called again.

"I can't believe you came!" Mildred gasped. "I can't believe they let you! I can't believe that Aunt *Oplisa* —"

"Permission for this one trip." Aunt Lilith smiled tightly. "She's controlling my broom."

Mildred swallowed. "Is it . . . true, then? That you're under a curse? Witch Fyrailn said —"

"Shh. We're starting."

Sure enough, Witch Harvigna had launched into a long, posturing speech about how amazing the Academy was. After several tedious minutes, Mildred's mind wandered, and she started peeking at all the families scattered around the clearing.

It was amazing how many male witches had been permitted here. Not just Rulisa's father, but Killyan's and Arzsanya's, several uncles, and even a grandfather squeezing Fiora's shoulder. It had been years since Mildred had seen a male witch, and she'd never spoken to one. Yet this all seemed so . . . so everyday to the rest of them.

Her heart squeezed with jealousy, watching Arzsanya and Killyan. Even Rulisa, who seemed to be fighting with her father in a furious undertone.

Just how sheltered was my upbringing? Mildred wondered uncertainly.

"Now, this," Witch Harvigna announced, holding up a tiny gold disc on a long chain, "is a blank talisman. Each of you will receive one before entering the Familiar Grove."

"Pay attention to this," Aunt Lilith murmured.

"You'll go alone," Witch Harvigna continued, "and emerge once you have seen your familiar. When you return, I'll record it here." She held up a thick, battered black book. "Understand?"

Aunt Lilith smirked slightly. "She really ought to go in with you. But of course she won't have the nerve. If she went in with you, you'd see her secrets, too."

"What did you get?" Mildred blurted out.

"I never came here." Aunt Lilith arched an eyebrow. "I went to Smoldering Institute."

Oops. She'd forgotten about that.

"But Oplisa got a kraken," Aunt Lilith said. "And Anklistine a chimera."

"What about Aunt Hurda?"

"They destroyed her talisman when they expelled her." Aunt Lilith looked sad. "Her magic's never been the same. I think she had a hellhound originally."

"Well?" Witch Harvigna called. "Who goes first?"

Nobody volunteered until Killyan's sister shoved her. Killyan yelped, flailed to keep her balance, and fell forward.

"Ah!" Witch Harvigna tossed the blank talisman at her. Killyan fumbled and missed, scrambling to the ground to pick it up. "Come back when it's ready."

Killyan looked around with wide, panicked eyes, but no one volunteered to take her place. At last, she stumbled to the clump of trees Witch Harvigna had indicated.

It took longer than Mildred expected. At first, everybody waited with baited breath. Then, as minutes stretched past, people started to resume their conversations.

"Yes," Aunt Lilith said quietly, breaking into Mildred's thoughts.

Mildred looked up, startled. "Huh?"

"Yes. We are cursed. By Oplisa."

Mildred swallowed. She didn't know how to ask. "Was it — was it back when — when Aunt Oplisa k-killed —?"

"Anklistine's sweetheart? Yes." Aunt Lilith's eyes darkened. "Nobody's supposed to kill witches, except their own death-enemy. But Oplisa doesn't care about policy."

Mildred swallowed. "So why doesn't anybody . . ."

"Stop her?" Aunt Lilith laughed hollowly. "Drakin did. They fought endlessly. They were fiercer rivals to each other than their own enemies. Now, however . . ."

"Everybody's afraid of her," Mildred whispered.

Aunt Lilith nodded. "Everybody's afraid of her."

"But Aunt Oplisa praises Drakin," Mildred protested. "Shouldn't that mean they were allies, not enemies?"

Aunt Lilith looked at her curiously. "You really don't understand rivalry, do you?"

Mildred shook her head.

Aunt Lilith sighed. "We use enemies to measure our own personal worth. Rivalry can be closer than friendship."

That makes no sense, Mildred thought heatedly.

Killyan finally stumbled out. "It's — it's a goblin!" she cried, holding up her gold talisman.

Several girls snickered. Her parents exchanged embarrassed looks.

"A *goblin?*" her older sister shrieked. "You're pathetic!"

Mildred gulped. She was glad Aunt Oplisa wasn't here.

Ainlar was sent next, then Keenlin. Laynan's mother noticed Aunt Lilith and cried out in recognition. Within two minutes, they were deep in conversation about old school days together. Mildred wandered off to look for Trasia.

She found her friend fighting with Gyrinal over whether rocs were superior to gryphons. Neither turned when she waved.

Would anybody notice if I volunteered to go next? Mildred wondered sourly.

At the furthest edge of the clearing, her eyes caught Rulisa and her father, still fighting in whispers. Curious, she snuck in that direction. They didn't seem to notice.

"I *said* I don't need it," Rulisa hissed, trying to shove something back at him. "I *told* you I'll be fine on my own."

"And I'm certain you won't," her father hissed.

"Do you have to cheat at *everything?*" Rulisa snarled.

Intrigued, Mildred stopped, but they didn't say any more. They just started shoving something at each other in silent fury.

Arzsanya emerged, squealing about a siren. Raginreln and Laynan broke into heated discussion over whether wyverns or hydras were more powerful.

"Mildred!" Trasia called, waving at her. "Get over here and tell Gyrinal that she's an idiot!"

Mildred volunteered to go next.

Stepping into the Familiar Grove, Mildred's mind whirled. It seemed to take a long time to focus her thoughts. But at last, she saw a flurry in the distance.

Wind brushed past her cheek, and she felt the drumming of cloven hooves. The breeze whirled in front of her, billowing into a translucent shape.

It looked faintly equine, but with a wild grace no horse ever had. Its horn was tipped with gold. Where the karkadann's mane had burned blue flame, the unicorn's blew transparent wind.

Then it was gone.

"Oh," Mildred whispered.

She looked at her talisman. It was no longer blank.

Aunt Lilith swooped down on her as soon as she walked out. "What is it?" she demanded, snatching the talisman.

Mildred tried to swallow the lump in her throat. "It's —"

"Why, it's a karkadann!" Aunt Lilith cried loudly. "What a fitting choice! Your mother's was a dragon, you know."

Mildred stared at her, stunned. A *karkadann?* How could anyone —

"Karkadann, eh?" Witch Harvigna murmured, coming over and glancing at it. She scribbled something in the huge book. "Odd for a wind witch. Still, if Drakin had a dragon, and they're arguably fire-based . . ."

Mildred snatched her talisman back, resentment burning. Her familiar was *not* a karkadann. Why had Aunt Lilith lied?

"Who's next?" Witch Harvigna called, stomping off.

"What'd you get?" Trasia cried, running over. "I hope it's not another goblin."

"Karkadann," Aunt Lilith said firmly.

Trasia squinted at Mildred's disc. "Are you sure?" she asked doubtfully. "'Cause it looks more like a —"

"*Karkadann,*" Aunt Lilith repeated.

Trasia stared at her a moment, looking puzzled. Then her eyes widened.

"Oh! Karkadann! Right!" She flung the talisman back as if it had burned her. "Definitely a karkadann."

"It's *not!*" Mildred cried. "It's —"

"White magic," Aunt Lilith said tensely, "is not permitted here."

Furious, Mildred jerked her head away. She saw Rulisa emerging from the thicket, her face ashen.

"What is it?" Witch Harvigna demanded.

Rulisa slowly pulled a talisman out of her pocket. "Nightbat," she muttered.

"Nightbat!" Witch Harvigna cried, scribbling it down. "Symbol of fire and darkness! Perfect!"

"Can I go back to class?" Rulisa asked flatly.

"No," Witch Harvigna snapped. "Wait until we're finished."

"What a snoooooob," Trasia groaned. "I'm glad she's not my enemy."

Aunt Lilith had gone still. "That's Mildred's death-enemy?"

"Yup!" Trasia bragged. "Most powerful witch in the school. Name's Rulisa. They've got a blood feud and everything."

Aunt Lilith's eyes darkened. "I need to speak with my niece alone."

Looking startled, Trasia stared at her. Aunt Lilith's eyes hardened. Trasia shrugged and headed back towards Gyrinal.

Aunt Lilith waited until Trasia was well out of earshot. Then she leaned forward, reaching into her pocket.

"Have you taken Elemental Reversal yet?" she whispered.

Puzzled, Mildred shook her head.

Aunt Lilith sighed. "Have you at least heard of wind-stones? Earth-songs? Fire-flowers? Water-patterns?"

Mildred shook her head.

"They're extremely rare," Aunt Lilith murmured. "Yet they can be cultivated. A talented composer may discover an earth-song. A brilliant alchemist could replicate a water-pattern. A clever linguist might encourage a wind-stone. And an unsurpassed gardener . . ."

She opened her fist. It held a tiny bud. Light flickered beneath its tight petals.

"Anklistine has grown her fifth one of these."

Mildred stared at the fire-flower, mesmerized.

"This gives the power of fire to all but those who have it naturally," Aunt Lilith said. "Those of its own element, it burns."

Mildred looked up, startled. "It *burns?*"

Aunt Lilith nodded sharply. "Take it. Use it. It's the perfect weapon against a fire witch: silent, unsuspected, deadly."

Mildred jerked back. "You wants me to . . . kill Rulisa?"

"Only if you can without getting caught," Aunt Lilith said fiercely. "Don't get expelled."

"I'm not going to do that!" Mildred was appalled. "Take it back. I don't want it!"

"I will not take it back," Aunt Lilith grated. "It burned me enough on my way here. Besides, do you want Oplisa to have one more of these?"

Mildred fell silent. "I'll take it," she said reluctantly.

"Thank you." Aunt Lilith dropped it in her palm, and visibly relaxed. She closed her eyes and let out a deep breath. "Now you have something to protect you."

Mildred clenched her teeth. *Not that I'll ever use it, even in an emergency.*

Chapter 10
The Group Assignment

Fourteen weeks, Mildred thought proudly. She had made it up to Basic Talismans in just fourteen weeks. And she'd even gotten Trasia advanced up with her!

"It's not worth the effort," Trasia had complained. "They're just going to fail me back down again."

But Mildred had made Trasia's advancement her personal crusade. She checked all of Trasia's homework, making her redo it if she had made any mistakes. She demanded extra credit and spent hours repeating teachers' lectures until her friend understood them. Trasia looked more ticked off about the whole thing every passing week, but she couldn't argue with the results — after only three weeks of intense extra credit, group projects, and hounding the teachers, Trasia was now up to her first-ever third-level class.

And I'm on my third! Mildred thought, thrilled.

Oh, she still failed back to Old Tongue Fundamentals occasionally, and she still hated Traditions, so she never got above the second level. But she'd just advanced to Basic Unraveling last week, and she was in fourth-level Witch History. Witch Khantar had even hinted that she might start Expert Witch History next week!

"Higher level means more homework," Trasia muttered, slouching down in her seat. "And you won't even let me skip doing it. Why'd we have to fight to be here?"

"We have to advance sometime to graduate," Mildred reminded her. "Now we're both closer to our aims!"

"*Our* aims?" Trasia asked incredulously. "I was perfectly fine with failing most weeks."

"No, you weren't," Mildred said, irritated. "You've been here two years and were first-level in practically everything. How did you ever expect to graduate?"

"You sound just like Heidanlar," Trasia muttered. "'Say thank you'—"

"I do *not!* I'm trying to help you!"

"Oh, gee," Trasia sneered. "I didn't realize there was such a difference. *Thank you.*"

Mildred spun around and faced front. She could barely contain her rage.

"This week," Witch Taelantri announced, "you will make group talismans together. Newest students, this might be your first talisman ever."

Mildred sat up straight and nodded excitedly.

"I've split you all into groups," Witch Taelantri went on. "Be creative and impress me. Yes, Raginreln?"

"Can we pick our own groups?" the skinny girl asked hopefully.

"No. I've already assigned them. Laynan?"

"I'm not going to be paired with an earth witch again, am I?" the fat girl demanded.

Witch Taelantri's expression grew pinched. "As a matter of fact, Killyan is in your group."

Laynan glared at Killyan. Her face went pale.

"The groups," Witch Taelantri went on shortly, "are, as follows: Killyan, Laynan, and Suzarx; Arzsanya, Raginreln, and Mildred; Trasia, Fiora, Ainlar, and Danyarsa; and Vaysa, Gyrinal, and Rulisa. Yes, Laynan?"

"Can't I switch places with Rulisa?" the fat girl whined. "I'd rather work with Gyrinal and Vaysa."

"I'm aware of that," Witch Taelantri snapped. "Why do you think I didn't put you with them again? Now, get to work! Start brainstorming! I want a project proposal from each group before we finish today!"

The girls split into groups, the room buzzing with activity. Rulisa didn't look up from her textbook as Vaysa stormed over to her.

Raginreln jabbed Mildred's arm. "Hey! New girl! We have a project to plan."

"If you flip to the back of your Talismans book, you'll see some ideas," Witch Taelantri called over the noise.

Arzsanya and Raginreln flipped to the back of their books. Arzsanya studied hers and looked up, clearing her throat.

"Okay," she said to Raginreln, "I'm water, you're fire, and she's wind. It seems to me we should do something weather-related."

"Like a storm, you mean?" Raginreln asked.

Arzsanya nodded.

"Hmmm . . ." Raginreln frowned. "Practically everybody's going to go weather-related. If we're going to brew a storm, it should be different somehow. Maybe lightning that seeks out specific people?"

"Ooh, great idea!" Arzsanya brightened. "Anyone you're hoping to get rid of?"

"Nah. Got no enemies." Raginreln shrugged. "But we could just tell it to kill the nearest Normal within certain parameters."

"Makes sense," Arzsanya said, grabbing a piece of paper and scribbling with her fingernail. Red ink appeared in curly handwriting.

"Um," Mildred said tentatively, "I don't like that idea —"

"Male, of course," Raginreln said, drumming her fingers on the table. "Probably commoner too, so no one would notice. Shall we say dark hair and dark eyes and somewhere near the edge of Forest Beyond, and leave it at that?"

"Makes sense to me," Arzsanya nodded, grabbing another piece of paper and scribbling. "I'd want to say no family too, though, in case he has a hero sister or something."

"Normal heroes are usually men, but yeah, good idea."

"I'm not going to help you kill somebody!" Mildred broke in.

"I'm not recommending killing a *witch*." Raginreln rolled her eyes.

"Yeah, and this will be more interesting," Arzsanya added.

Mildred clenched her teeth. "I'm not — going to help you — kill somebody," she repeated.

"Are you *crazy?*" Vaysa's voice shrieked across the room. "That's the stupidest idea I've ever heard!"

Every head turned to stare at her.

"What's stupid about summoning a firebird?" Rulisa demanded, her ears red. "They're powerful, and two fire witches and one wind witch would make for the ideal —"

"Well, for starters, they're related to *phoenixes!*"

Rulisa's ears turned crimson. "And karkadanns are related to unicorns. What's your point?"

"I like Vaysa's idea," Gyrinal said loyally. "Volcanos are more interesting than birds."

"We'd need an earth witch to make a volcano," Rulisa said through clenched teeth. "You're wind."

"Oh, so our idea *couldn't* work!" Vaysa cried. "You think you're so superior, but you're *not!* You were raised by a *man,* in case you've forgotten!"

Rulisa's ears trailed smoke. "My father is far more powerful than you'll ever be."

"You're nothing," Vaysa hissed. "I could kill you right now."

Rulisa snorted derisively.

"You'd get expelled if you did!" Gyrinal cried, looking frightened. "Killing's forbidden on Academy grounds, Vaysa!"

Mildred looked frantically at the teacher, but Witch Taelantri was just watching, lips curled with amusement.

"Okay," Vaysa said quietly, "then I won't kill you. Maybe I'll just singe you a bit."

"Apparently you're stupid." Rulisa looked bored. "I'm a fire witch, too."

"Mildred! Gyrinal!" Vaysa shouted, spinning around. "Suffocate her!"

Mildred gaped at her. "Are you *insane?*"

"I'm not going to get expelled for killing!" Gyrinal squeaked.

Rulisa snorted. "Wow. A coward who can't even fight for herself. Now I'm really scared."

Vaysa snarled and lunged. She seized Rulisa by the throat and caught her in a chokehold.

"I've killed five Normals this way," Vaysa snarled. "Let's see how magic helps you out of this, little miss know-it-all!"

Mildred leapt up to stop them, but Vaysa waved her free arm, and flames exploded all around them.

Rulisa's face turned purple. She thrashed, not breaking free.

Witch Taelantri was still watching with mild interest.

"SOMEBODY *DO* SOMETHING!" Mildred shouted.

"Is she actually going to die?" an older girl asked curiously.

Witch Taelantri shrugged. "Maybe. Harvigna would thank me."

"Raginreln!" Mildred gasped. "You're a fire witch! You can get through those flames! You save —"

"Are you nuts?" Raginreln asked incredulously. "Nobody here likes Rulisa."

Fire. Mildred's hand flew to her pocket. *I have something that could get through —*

She didn't stop to think. She grabbed the fire-flower bud and threw it straight at Vaysa.

"BLOOM!" she shouted.

The tiny bud blazed through the flames and landed right on Vaysa's arm. For a second, nothing happened. Then petals exploded, and Vaysa started screaming.

"GET IT OFF ME! GET IT OFF ME!"

Rulisa gasped and fell to the ground.

A spiky vine lashed from the flower and slashed at Vaysa's face. She grabbed for it, screaming as it burned her, and it lunged around her neck and started to squeeze.

"Get off!" Mildred screamed, horrified. She dove for Vaysa and snatched at the petals. "Get off her!"

The flower came loose in her hands, wilting as she touched it. The petals collapsed into tiny embers. The vine turned to ash.

"Get it off, get it off," Vaysa sobbed, still clutching her arm. There were boiling red welts everywhere the flower had been. Witch Taelantri stalked over and pried her fingers away.

"No permanent damage," she said matter-of-factly. "Well, maybe a little. But you'll live."

Vaysa collapsed to the ground, still sobbing.

"Oh, stop sniveling and get to your dorm," Witch Taelantri said, looking unsympathetic. "These things happen. In fact, you should thank her. You would have been expelled if you'd succeeded."

Vaysa stumbled to her feet. She looked up at Mildred and gave her a livid glare. Then she burst into tears all over again and ran from the room.

There was silence in the classroom as Rulisa stumbled to her feet, coughed hard, and collapsed back into her chair.

"I guess we can reassign groups for the week," Witch Taelantri sighed. "Ainlar, take Vaysa's place. And *you* . . ."

Mildred flinched as the teacher spun and glared at her.

"Would you mind explaining why you protected your enemy?" she asked coldly.

Chapter 11

Two Liars

ringing, Mildred entered the High Witch's bedroom. It was decorated in torture instruments, and its low ceilings were covered in frescos to illustrate the many uses of these.

"H-High Witch?" she stammered. "Witch Taelantri s-sent me here."

A shadow flickered across the wall. A black cat leapt from the ceiling and landed in front of her. It melted into the dark form of High Witch Tractia.

"Ah," she murmured, tucking a small gold disc under her robes. "Did you try to kill your death-enemy?"

Mildred shook her head, mute. She hadn't known the High Witch's familiar was a shadow-panther. She certainly hadn't realized they could learn to take the shapes of their familiars.

High Witch Tractia sighed. "Pity. What *did* you do?"

"I — I — well, sort of the opposite," Mildred stammered. "I stopped Vaysa from killing her."

Silence as the High Witch pondered this.

"You protected your death-enemy," she said at last, slowly. "How idiotic."

"Vaysa was going to kill her!" Mildred cried.

"Mmm . . . I suppose it would have been a waste to expel Vaysa. Not to mention losing Rulisa. But that would be a teacher's reason. Why did *you* intervene?"

Mildred swallowed. She remembered what Aunt Lilith had told her three weeks ago. Somehow, she doubted that *because it was the right thing to do* was going to fly here.

Think, she thought frantically. *How would Aunt Anklistine answer such a question?*

"I couldn't . . . let someone else kill her," Mildred said slowly. "Rulisa's *my* enemy. How would that look for me?"

The High Witch smiled faintly. "True. But was antagonizing Vaysa worth it?"

"I didn't say I actually thought it through," Mildred muttered.

"Careful." The High Witch's eyes darkened. "You might remind me of somebody else. *'I can't possibly be content with just one enemy, High Witch, I'm so strong I need at least three . . .'*"

Mildred jerked back, startled. The High Witch's imitation of Aunt Oplisa had sounded eerily accurate.

"That attitude is both greedy and arrogant. I will not tolerate it."

Mildred stared at the High Witch, stunned. *She thinks I was trying to make* more *enemies?*

"I promise I won't deliberately antagonize Vaysa again," she said fervently. "One enemy's enough for me."

"Good." The High Witch looked pleased. "Then I will let you off with a warning."

Mildred felt lightheaded with relief. The last student High Witch Tractia had punished had stayed blind for a week. She glanced longingly at the exit.

"However . . ."

Mildred turned back, her heart pounding. "Y-yes?"

"Don't forget that Rulisa *is* your enemy," High Witch Tractia said quietly. "Never mistake rivalry for friendship."

Mildred gulped. "Y-yes, High Witch."

"Then go." High Witch Tractia waved her hand. "Oh, and incidentally . . . congratulations."

"Congratulations?"

"Assuming someone graduates and you flunk nothing, you'll make Fourth Class next week."

Startled, Mildred watched the High Witch melt back into a shadow-panther. The black cat leapt up the wall and vanished into the darkness. Mildred stared at the empty space for a long minute before remembering where she was and fleeing the room.

I never thought to calculate the class rankings. I've only been here for half a year.

Does this mean I've been advancing as quickly as my enemy?

She should have felt flattered at the news. She should have been delighted. But somehow, the idea just made her feel sick.

I used to be scared I'd fail everything, she thought, chewing her lower lip as she walked past a frozen griffin. She was heading back to her dorm, instead of to Menacing Spells. *Yet now I'm excelling. Shouldn't I be happy? Shouldn't I at least feel . . . relieved?*

But she didn't. She felt appalled. Dirty.

Mildred touched the tiny gold disc she wore underneath her dress every day.

Ashamed.

Unicorns were almost as pure white magic as tennin or phoenixes. No matter what the others would think, she had felt proud of this. And she knew — she *knew* — her familiar didn't belong here. If she started to excel here . . . that would be like a betrayal.

I don't want to do this! her mind exploded. *I don't want Aunt Oplisa proud of me! I don't want to be some great success story for this school! I don't want them to take* any *credit for my learning!*

Mildred reached the open door to her dorm, and froze. Rulisa was sitting at the back of the room.

Black hair cascaded over her tense shoulders and onto the pages she was reading. She jerked up at the noise.

"*You!*"

Mildred waved sheepishly.

"Why are you here?" Rulisa snarled. "Come to taunt about saving me?"

Mildred swallowed. "Wh-why aren't you in class?"

"I didn't feel like heading off to Merciless Spells," Rulisa said, looking surly. "Given that someone just tried to kill me. What's your excuse?"

Mildred gulped. Crazily, she wanted to admit the truth. Or at least, the part of it that didn't involve High Witch Tractia.

"I — I had a fight with Trasia. I kind of . . . didn't want to face her. I thought I was being a good friend, but . . ."

Rulisa snorted. "How nice for you."

"Was I a bad friend?" Mildred blurted out.

Rulisa stared at her incredulously. "Why would you ask me?"

"Because . . . other than Trasia . . . you're the closest thing I have to . . ."

"I am *not!* I'm your *enemy!*"

"Aunt Lilith told me rivalry can be closer than friendship."

Rulisa squeezed her eyes shut, clenching her teeth. Mildred noticed she was shaking, and the bruises all around her neck looked red and swollen.

"Are you all right?" she asked quietly.

Rulisa's eyes snapped open. "My death-enemy just saved me. What do you think?"

"You know I don't want to be enemies."

"Saving me was stupid enough," Rulisa snarled. "Saying that in front of anyone else would be a dead giveaway."

Mildred blinked. "About . . . ?"

"Karkadann, my foot. You got a buraq or unicorn."

Mildred jerked back. "How could you —?"

"Karkadanns symbolize vengeance. You can't even wrap your mind around a blood feud."

"Well, what about you?" Mildred asked heatedly. "You're no nightbat! You're a liar, too!"

Rulisa's ears slowly turned red. "Don't you dare call me that."

"Why not? Nightbats symbolize deceivers. You should think that's a compliment."

Rulisa's ears darkened to crimson.

"What did you do," Mildred asked, "show them your mother's talisman?"

"Of . . . course not."

"Then why did I see your father give it to you?"

Rulisa's jaw clenched.

"Why are you even here?" Mildred demanded. "Did your father make you come, or something?"

"No," Rulisa muttered. "It was my choice."

"Then why —"

Rulisa leapt up and slammed her textbook against the wall.

"*My mother's dead, okay?*" she shouted. "The only chance I have to understand her is to follow in her footsteps! And that's all because of *your* family!"

She stormed out, ears exploding smoke and lightning.

She wants to follow in her mother's footsteps? Mildred wondered, dumbfounded. *Why? I want nothing to do with mine.*

Chapter 12

Punishment

aysa spent the next seven weeks trying to make Mildred's life miserable.

She destroyed every piece of homework she could find, sabotaged half her class assignments, and even deliberately failed down two classes just to torment her more effectively.

One night, Mildred's mattress even exploded.more effectively.

And then Mildred's mattress exploded.

It was only by pure chance she had put her slippers down before sitting herself. That trap, and her incinerated slippers, convinced her that she needed magical protection.

Thankfully, Witch Fyrailn had agreed to teach her wards.

"They're really not taught until eighth-level Elements," she had said in her clipped voice, "but I think you can handle it. Drakin was an expert at these."

Hurray.

Fortunately, Trasia had proved less capable of holding a grudge, which was the only bright spot of the second week.

Mildred was sitting at breakfast alone, pushing bites of food around on her plate, when another tray plopped in front of her.

"Hi," Trasia said without preamble. "So, life's boring here without friends, not to mention miserable. Truce?"

Mildred's mouth fell open. "T-truce!"

"Great." Trasia sat down.

Mildred gulped her bite of omelet. "Um . . . how are your classes?"

"Horrid," Trasia said cheerfully. "Gonna fail 'em all down again."

Mildred waited for Trasia to ask for her help. She didn't.

"I asked Witch Dhadia the Old Tongue word for 'shrimp,'" Mildred said tentatively.

"Great," Trasia said. "What is it?"

"*Biffin.*"

"*Drakon biffin,*" Trasia said hopefully to her tray.

The cracked tray sprouted three chunks of green meat and a handful of undercooked shrimp.

"Ugh," Trasia muttered, poking at it. "That's just wrong, you stupid tray."

"I'm . . . I'm sorry I tried to control your class schedule," Mildred said, choking a little on the words. "I just . . . wanted us to be in the same classes."

"Yup," Trasia said. "You made that clear already."

"And I wanted . . ."

"Mildred." Trasia slammed her fork down. "Look. I'm not *trying* to fail things. But I gotta do things at my own pace, and that doesn't happen to be your pace. So just eat your food and shut up, okay?"

Gulping, Mildred went back to her alligator pancakes.

With Trasia by her side, school seemed so much better. She accepted her promotion to Fourth Class without any further worries, and her hatred of the school dimmed even further when she advanced two more classes in the space of one week. Intermediate Elements *and* Expert Witch History!

"Witch Granwir claims I lack the aggression to make it in Frightening Spells," Mildred bounced as they walked towards the dinner hall, "but I bet I can advance anyway as soon as some other teacher gets the class. I get the best homework averages every week."

"Mmm-hm," Trasia muttered.

"And I'm even learning how to not burn everything in Cauldron Usages," Mildred chattered excitedly as they entered the dinner hall. It looked the same as the breakfast hall, except that it had statues and dim lighting, and the tables were in neat rows instead of strewn randomly.

"I might even advance to Basic Brews next week! Which means I'd be in *three* third-level classes, one fourth-level, one *fifth*-level —"

"Yeah, yeah." Trasia looked bored. "All bottom for me again, I'm sure, but we'll find out tomorrow. Can we talk about something else now, please?"

"I even made my first bauble yesterday," Mildred went on, hopping up and down. "They're like charms, only you wear them like jewelry, and they affect yourself instead of other people, and they can be used for all kinds of things . . ."

"What was this, a chatter-bauble?" Trasia asked in exasperation. "Stop talking!"

"EVERYONE!" High Witch Tractia's voice boomed across the dinner hall. "DINNER IS CANCELED! ASSEMBLE AT THE OFFICIAL HALL!"

Mildred jumped, startled. "Wh-what's the official hall?"

"Thingy," Trasia said, shrugging.

"Um — where is it?"

Trasia pointed at the stack of trays, which were dissolving into black goo. "Right here."

Mildred watched, feeling sick, as the rest of the room liquified around them. The tables and chairs melted into sticky black mounds, then exploded into thirteen rows of thirteen seats. She yelped as one burst in front of her and spattered across her face.

"See?" Trasia said.

"Wow," Mildred whispered. "Why don't we see this more often?"

"High Witch uses it for graduations," Trasia shrugged. "Teachers and First Class are the only ones who usually go."

Mildred scrubbed the goop off her face and dropped it on the floor, where it sizzled and slurped into the stone. She looked up as the front of the room bulged into a stage.

High Witch Tractia mounted the stage as the last details formed — a pattern of scales across the front, two pillars covered in tiny statues, and a flickering chandelier — then stood expectantly in the center. A table erupted behind her and seethed into a squat metallic cauldron.

Students and teachers were hurrying through the doorway. Witch Felspan counted and finally nodded up to the stage. As the last few students settled into remaining empty seats, she joined the other teachers in front of the exit.

Mildred snuck a peek at Rulisa, several rows behind them. Her death-enemy looked tense.

"Black Magic Academy," High Witch Tractia said loudly, as the cauldron's foam spilled across the stage, "is a school with a long tradition of greatness. This is largely because we are so selective about students we accept here to begin with. But we also have another method to weed out the less . . . apt."

Mildred's mouth went dry. Surely that didn't mean . . .

"EXPULSION!"

Mildred grabbed the edge of her chair. She looked back at Rulisa, whose knuckles had gone white.

"Come forward, Trasia, daughter of Maronela and Torantun."

Mildred's mouth fell open. She turned and stared at her friend.

Trasia?

Trasia looked frozen.

TRASIA?

Slowly, Trasia stood.

TRASIA?!

Mildred gaped wordlessly as her only friend walked up to the stage and stood in front of the High Witch.

"You are a disgrace to the name of witchcraft," High Witch Tractia hissed. "You've failed every single bottom class this week. After two years of education here! Have you nothing to say for yourself?"

Trasia lifted her chin proudly. "I know why you're doing this. It's not because I've failed things. It's because I'm a village witch."

"One notess that thiss village witch became a teacher!" Witch Hoiyanar called.

The High Witch snatched the badge from Trasia's chest and flung it at the cauldron. It shattered.

She seized the familiar talisman off her neck. It exploded.

"BEGONE!" she shouted.

A hole erupted through the back of the stage. The floor dissolved under Trasia's feet and swallowed her in a river of sticky goo.

Mildred leapt to her feet. *"NO!"* she screamed.

The goo whirlpooled through the hole and slurped closed.

"And thus is our school purified," High Witch Tractia said with satisfaction.

"*NO!*" Mildred screamed again.

The High Witch smacked the wall, which shivered and began dissolving again. In a moment, the dinner hall was reforming.

Mildred simply slithered to the floor when her seat melted, and stayed there.

No, she thought numbly. *They couldn't. They couldn't expel her. How can they get rid of my only friend?*

"I hate expulsions," one older girl complained, pushing past.

"I know," another girl sighed, wiping black goo off her fingers. "The school gets so surly. I know we can't just let it eat them, but it really wants to."

"Yeah, well, can't let it get a taste for students, Witch Fyrailn says. Not even the worthless ones."

"You're so lucky you got into her History of the Academy class! I'm still stuck with History of the Forest Beyond!"

Mildred didn't move. She couldn't. Life without Trasia seemed desperately lonely.

"It makes sense, you know," Rulisa said, standing over her.

"Makes *sense?!*" Mildred screamed, jumping to her feet. "How could you *say* that?!"

"She never bothered to work. Frankly, I'm shocked it didn't happen years earlier."

"You barely know her!" Mildred screamed. "She's my *friend!*"

"True," Rulisa said. "I pick my friends more carefully than you do."

"You don't *have* any friends!"

"Yeah, well," Rulisa said vaguely. "I'll see you tomorrow in Witch History."

Mildred buried her face in her hands and cried.

Chapter 13
Broomstick vs. Mildred

uietly, a shadow moved into the doorway. Witch Dhadia was halfway through her lecture before she realized it was there.

"H-High Witch Tractia!" she gasped. "For what reason do we — ahem — owe this honor?"

The shadow lurched into the shape of the High Witch. She stood there, looking faintly contemptuous. "I've come to fetch one of your students."

Witch Dhadia stared at her. "One of . . . ?"

"To run an errand for me."

Gasps rang around the classroom. Several of the girls started to chatter excitedly.

"No!" Witch Dhadia cried, looking harassed. "High Witch, surely you realize that preparing make-up work for any student is a difficult job. I'm busy enough already —"

"Hush," the High Witch snapped. "Mildrin will be gone the rest of the week. There's no need to bother."

Witch Dhadia brightened. "Oh! Then one less student to rank!"

Mildrin? Mildred looked up from her cauldron. *Does she mean me?*

"You." The High Witch jabbed a finger at her. "This way."

Mildred's stomach plummeted. *She does mean me.*

Reluctantly, she headed past the disappointed murmurs, out into the hallway. Her mind was racing. *Why me? Is this because I've gone down in half of my classes since Trasia was expelled? I haven't been slacking, I've just been . . .*

Trasia.

Gloom washed over Mildred again. The past two weeks had been miserable. It had been bad enough when she and Trasia were fighting — now, she didn't even know where Trasia lived.

Not to mention that the newest girl seemed to worship Heidanlar. That didn't help matters.

High Witch Tractia paused between two statues of a snarling oxenbeast and cyclops holding a thorny whip. Those two had been hovering near the Witch History classrooms all week.

"How well can you ride a broomstick?" she asked curiously.

"How well can I *ride a broomstick?*" Mildred asked in horror.

"Answer the question, don't repeat it," High Witch Tractia snapped.

Mildred gulped. "I — I — I don't know, High Witch. Not very well, I think."

Really wretchedly horribly, actually.

The High Witch looked irritated. "Then I will control it for you. This way."

She strode through the wall beside the statue. Mildred hesitated for a second, then followed her into cluttered, dusty room. It was full of broomsticks. Shabby, stout, new, dull, garish . . . every type of broomstick Mildred had ever seen.

"I have two errands for you," the High Witch said coolly as she selected a sleek model from a hook above their heads. "The first should only take a few hours — or days, if your luck's poor. The second will take longer. You'll be staying at the Smoldering Institute."

Mildred's eyes widened. "Smoldering Institute?" she gasped. "Why are you sending me there? I'm not a fire witch!"

The High Witch smirked. "Exactly. They'll have to let down their shields to get you in. My spy-spells may be able to sneak through when you do."

Mildred touched her forehead. "But — but why me?"

"Three reasons." High Witch Tractia dropped the broomstick to the ground. "First: you're barely Fourth Class. That is both an insult to them and a reason for you to be underestimated. Second: you come from an extremely powerful family. That means you have hidden potential that they may not expect. Third: your ownership of that fire-flower fascinates me. If you have any chance of 'finding' more of those before you visit . . ." High Witch Tractia smirked. "Well, use your imagination."

Mildred swallowed. Witch Taelantri had grilled her endlessly about the fire-flower, trying to learn where she'd gotten it. High Witch Tractia had not, which led her to suspect she'd already guessed. Everybody knew Aunt Anklistine's reputation for gardening.

"Now, your first errand." The High Witch Tractia pulled a black piece of paper from her pocket and wedged it tightly in the bristles. "You'll go directly to the giantess Jurunheir. Deliver this message."

"*Giantess?*" Mildred gasped.

"Correct."

"But — but —" Mildred fumbled for words. "Why a *giantess?*"

"To deliver my message." High Witch Tractia looked annoyed. "Do try listening. Oh, and attempt to avoid the husband. He eats humans."

"He *WHAT?*"

"Sit," the High Witch ordered, pointing at the broomstick.

Mildred swallowed. "I — I'd really rather stay here," she warbled. "I'm behind in my classwork, and I really don't think —"

"I don't care what you think." The High Witch pointed again. "Sit."

Mildred gulped and obeyed.

"You." High Witch Tractia pinched the broom's bristles in her sharp fingernails. "You will take the witch now seated on you to the Mist-Enshrouded Castle. After that, the Smoldering Institute. No delays, no detours, no dropping. Go!"

The broom leapt to the ceiling. Mildred yelped, clutching the bristles. High Witch Tractia snapped, and a window splattered open ahead of them.

"Take as long as you need, but no longer!" the High Witch called after them.

Mildred squeezed her eyes shut and clung to the bristles, terrified. She hated flying. Hated flying. *Hated* flying.

She forced herself to peek down after a few minutes, then found the view so spectacular that she almost forgot she was dangling so far over it.

The Forest Beyond stretched for miles and miles, tree after tree of brilliant green. The occasional tiny clearings were carpeted in flowers and thornbushes, and the highest branches snatched towards the sky as if trying to reach them.

"Wow," Mildred whispered.

She barely noticed as the air got thinner — it clustered around a wind witch's head naturally, anyway — and drank in the view until they finally reached the forest limits. Trees dwindled into bushes, scrubby flatland, and then finally they passed a tiny farming community.

Mildred was squinting at the cliff beside the farmland, trying to figure out why there were tiny green lines running up it, when the broomstick took a sharp dive.

Mildred shrieked.

They zoomed towards an enormous castle which lurked at the edge of the cliff. Just far enough away to be annoying, the broom dumped her into a thick spray of grass.

"*Ow!*" Mildred complained, glaring up at it.

The broomstick stood itself on end, looking smug.

Grumbling, Mildred stood up, brushed off her clothes, took a deep breath, and almost walked right into a ditch.

Chapter 14

Beanstalks

Just in time, she yelped and leapt back from the enormous, dry moat. "You put me on the wrong side!" she accused the broom.

It leapt up eagerly.

"Oh, no you don't," Mildred said darkly. "I'll get across it myself."

The broom spun incredulously.

Mildred got on her knees and peered over the edge of the ditch. Sure enough, there were thick green vines here too. She hadn't had much experience with climbing, but she was definitely better at it than flying, and this ditch was a lot wider than it was tall. She rubbed her hands in dirt and prepared to descend.

"Oh, now the mayor's sending *novices* after me?" a rude voice exclaimed.

Mildred leapt back from the edge, startled. An indignant-looking man was standing behind her.

"W-who . . . ?" she began.

"That should be *my* question!" he retorted. "Do you even *come* from Jacksville?"

"N-no . . ." Mildred said hesitantly.

"Typical." The man folded his arms. "It's my week to rob the giants. Take a number, like everyone else, and just wait your turn."

Mildred stared at him in astonishment. "But I'm not —"

The man shoved her aside and scaled the thick vine with practiced efficiency.

The broomstick leapt up and hovered in her face.

"All right, all right," Mildred sighed. "I'll ride you in. But if you drop me again, I'm telling the High Witch."

The carpet inside the castle was coarse and deep, and reminded her of the fast-growing grass she used to walk through before Aunt Anklistine did the weeding. Of course, it was thicker than grass; also softer. And mauve.

"TWELVE GOLD PIECES FOR AN EXTERMINATOR!"

Mildred gasped and leapt back. A gigantic foot had landed two feet from her.

"STOP COMPLAINING," a woman's voice snapped. The ground shook as a skirt and pair of laced-up boots stomped in from another room. "I TALKED HIM DOWN FROM NEARLY FIFTEEN, YOU KNOW."

"*TWELVE GOLD PIECES!*"

Mildred swallowed, ducking down into the carpet. She was supposed to deliver a letter to — *that?*

"WOULD YOU RATHER HAVE PESTS ROBBING YOU EVERY WEEK?"

"AT LEAST THE PESTS CAN'T CARRY GOLD PIECES!"

Mildred clutched her hands over her ears, in pain from the noise. The broom rocked from side to side, looking bored. Mildred yanked her hands off her ears long enough to shove it back into the carpet. Looking annoyed, the broom shot straight towards the ceiling.

"AT LEAST EXTERMINATORS ARE —" The giantess's voice stopped abruptly. Mildred held her breath, her eyes fastened on the broom, which was now turning cartwheels behind the giant's head. What did it think it was *doing?*

"DEAREST," the giantess said in a soothing voice, "YOU'VE HAD SUCH A LONG DAY. I'M SURE YOU'RE HUNGRY. I'VE MADE ONE OF YOUR FAVORITE STEWS FOR YOU IN THE KITCHEN."

The giant's voice sounded suspicious. "ARE YOU HARBORING ANOTHER PEST BECAUSE YOU'RE MAD AT ME?"

The giantess's voice became cloyingly sweet. "NOW, WHY WOULD YOU EVER SUSPECT SUCH A THING?"

Mildred put her face in her hands.

"WHAT KIND OF STEW?" The giant's legs moved, his sandal grazing Mildred's shoulder as he lifted it. "IT'S NOT POISONED AGAIN, IS IT?"

"NOW, DEAREST, WHEN HAVE I EVER —"

"LAST WEEK! AFTER WE FOUGHT ABOUT THE —"

"I THOUGHT WE AGREED THAT WAS AN ACCIDENT!"

"ONE OF US AGREED," the giant grumbled, thundering out of the room.

There was silence for a moment. Then the giantess ducked down and whispered, "Human! Human pest-thing! Why do you have a broomstick?"

Mildred swallowed and peered over the top of the carpet.

"Um —" she began.

"There you are!"

Mildred squeaked as the giantess's fingers reached out and grabbed her. She held her up to the light, squinting at her face.

"Haven't seen you before," the giantess murmured finally. "Such a scrawny little thing to have climbed all that way, too. Unless you flew up by broomstick?"

Mildred nodded quickly.

"Witch, then. I hate witches."

Hastily, Mildred yanked the broom towards her and tugged at the letter. It was wedged too tightly to come out.

The giantess eyed her. "What's that?"

"DID YOU SAY SOMETHING?" the giant's voice roared from another room.

"NOTHING, SWEETEST!" the giantess shot back.

Mildred winced and covered her ears.

"I'M FEEDING THAT STEW TO YOUR PET HUMANS RIGHT NOW, SO IT HAD BETTER NOT BE POISONED!"

"I TOLD YOU, IT ISN'T!"

The giantess sniffed and turned back to Mildred. "Well?" she whispered. "What's that?"

"It's a letter," Mildred said nervously. "From my High Witch. She — she wants to ask your help with something, I think."

"Letter," the giantess murmured. "You'd better enlarge it."

Hoping she remembered all the words correctly, Mildred chanted the enlarging spell she'd learned in Menacing Spells recently. Thankfully, it worked, and the black paper grew until it spilled out of the bristles and across the giantess's wrists.

"Stop," the giantess said. "That's big enough."

She dropped Mildred into an enormous vase containing several decorative trees, then squinted at the red handwriting.

"What's it say?" Mildred asked nervously, her voice echoing up the walls of the vase.

"Hmf." The giantess wadded the letter and tossed it at a pile of trash across the room. From her vantage point, Mildred could see that these giants were not meticulous housekeepers. There were almost as many piles of trash as there were chunks of gold lying everywhere. She was starting to see how humans could sneak in and make off with treasure regularly.

"ONE OF YOUR PET HUMANS DIED!" the giant's voice roared. "THIS STEW *IS* POISONED!"

The giantess jumped, making the whole floor rattle. She seized the broomstick from the air and shoved it down the vase at Mildred.

"You go back," she hissed, "and tell your High Witch to stop bothering me. I'm sick of her letters asking me to squash enemies. Now get out of here before my husband comes back, you understand?"

Mildred grabbed the broomstick, which zoomed upwards while she was still dangling. She hung on with both arms and fought a scream. The last thing she heard as the broomstick zipped away was the giantess marching back towards the kitchen, shouting, "NOW, DEAREST, I'M SURE THE THING WAS SICK ANYWAY . . ."

Mildred clung to the broom's handle, her hands slippery with sweat. They were skimming so near the trees of the Forest Beyond, high branches were snapping at her ankles. And she was still dangling.

"Broom!" she called, "let me up! This is dangerous!"

The broom slowed, looking reluctant. She grabbed the bristles.

It shot straight up and started bucking and thrashing.

"What are you, *ticklish?*" Mildred screamed. "Let me back up! My arms are slipping!"

The broom hesitated for half a second. She seized the bristles and struggled to pull herself up.

The broom held still. Then it jerked out of her grip and zoomed on without her.

Mildred's mouth gaped open in frozen fear.

Then trees came up to meet her.

Then nothing.

Chapter 15
The Forest Beyond

ubbing her head, Mildred sat up blearily. Head hurt. Sore all over. And where was she?

Trees coming up while I fell asleep . . .

Mildred jumped to her feet, alarmed. She hadn't fallen asleep — she'd *fallen!*

Panicking, she yanked everything out of her pockets. Did she have that directional charm with her? She'd made it back when she and Trasia were fighting . . .

Mildred found it in a snarl of classwork from Basic Talismans, and breathed a sigh of relief. She quickly set out to detangle everything.

Depression charm. She wrenched the sticky goo away, scrubbing it off against a tree. The only thing it had ever depressed was her hope of advancing that week.

Rage charm. She'd messed that one up deliberately. She'd been paired with Vaysa, and the last thing she had wanted was to make Vaysa more angry.

Tension charm. Mildred squinted at it. Probably the last thing she needed right now. She pushed the round ball out and shoved it in her pocket.

Darkness charm. Mildred perked up. She'd done a good job on that one! It even looked impressive, loops of knotted ribbon and string. Of course . . . in an increasingly dark forest . . . it would probably not be too helpful . . .

Mildred sighed and looked down at the final charm, which was completely tangled with it. The directional charm had never worked properly, which was why she'd quit using it weeks back, but it was better than nothing. Carefully, she looped and teased the metal chain until she'd gotten it free. Then she wrapped it around her hand.

"Find me the nearest human settlement," she ordered.

The charm snatched Mildred's wrist and leapt forward. She stumbled, nearly ran into a tree, and dodged just in time to continue a breakneck pace towards the charm's intended destination.

"NOT SO QUICKLY!" she shouted.

Naturally, it ignored her.

"Do — not — run — me — in — to — things!" she added as they dodged several more trees and picked up even more speed.

Naturally, it ignored this too.

Up ahead, Mildred saw a clearing. She barely had time to squeeze her eyes shut as they barreled right past a tree —

Flump. The charm fell limp in her hands.

Mildred looked down at it incredulously.

"This is not our destination," she informed it.

"*YAAAAAAAAAAAAA!*"

Mildred yelped, dodged, and whatever-it-was fell right by her.

It didn't succeed in missing the ground.

"*Owwwwwwwww,*" the bundle of fancy clothes complained, picking itself up. It seemed to contain a girl, several years older than Mildred, with flaming red hair and long, styled curls. In the fading twilight, it was difficult to see more detail than this.

"Are you okay?" Mildred asked uncertainly.

The girl brushed her hair back from her face and glared. "I'd be better if you hadn't dodged."

"I wouldn't have."

"So what? You're trying to rob me!"

"No —" Mildred began.

"That's it!" the girl cried, snatching her satchel from the ground. "Father sent you after me! I should have known he'd find a better tracker after the last time I ran away!"

Mildred stared at her. "Um . . ."

"Oh, all right," the girl sighed, opening the satchel. "I'm sure you forgot to bring food, just like the last eight. Honestly, you'd think soldiers would have a little more sense."

"I'm not a —"

"You'd think Father would get the hint, wouldn't you?" the girl continued furiously, rooting through the satchel. "I mean, seriously, a *frog* for a suitor? What was he *thinking?*"

"I've never met —"

"Just because some witch turned that duke's son into a frog on his way to —"

"You're courting a *marquess?*"

The girl stopped, staring at her. "Don't you know who I am?"

"Um," Mildred said. "No?"

"For crying out loud," the girl muttered. "I'm Topaz Sardion Angelica Rentav. Your princess."

Mildred's eyes widened. "My *what?*"

"And I hereby order you to speak to nobody about seeing me," Topaz added grandly.

"We have a *princess?*"

Topaz looked annoyed. "How could you possibly not know that?"

"I skipped Current Events," Mildred admitted. "It's first-level Witch History."

"Every commoner knows —"

"I'm not a commoner. I'm aristocracy."

"Got a title?"

"No —"

"Then you're a commoner."

"I'm not a village witch!"

Silence. Topaz eyed the charm in her hand.

"You're a . . . witch," she said slowly.

Mildred nodded.

"And you're telling me they think they've got their own *aristocracy?*" Topaz's voice rose. "They think they're *that* exempt from Father's laws? How dare they!"

Mildred gulped.

"No wonder Dad can never find the powerful ones," Topaz muttered.

"They must all keep hidden. He's going to love this . . ."

Mildred clutched her directional charm.

"Oh, don't worry, I don't care what you are," Topaz yawned. "My best friend's dating a witch, not that Father knows it. And Dorian's *real* aristocracy, too, not this made-up, title-less thing. What's your name?"

"Mildred —"

Topaz made a face. "That sounds like someone's grandmother's name."

"It *was* my grandmother's name."

"Figures. My family's got dumb naming traditions, too. All princesses get named after gemstones, but the good names were used centuries ago, and Dad has this thing against repetition, so guess who had to get a leftover idea that nobody else wanted? At least he didn't call me 'Sugilite.' He was considering it."

"Do you know the way out of the forest?" Mildred asked tentatively. "I was heading . . ."

"Not in the dark. Ask me in the morning."

Mildred stared at her.

"Because I'll be sleeping in that tree." Topaz pointed. "To keep nocturnal monsters from eating me."

Mildred kept on staring at her.

"Which means you can stay here," Topaz went on impatiently. "Pick a tree, any tree."

Mildred shuddered. Heights were terrifying enough when she was awake.

"I can cast wards," she remembered with relief, looping the directional charm back in her pocket. "Those can keep both of us safe."

The princess looked dubious. "I'm keeping the tree."

Mildred hesitated, then decided this would be as good a place to stay as any. She walked to the edge of the clearing and started murmuring Old Tongue words. She pinched the air in thirteen spots and traced a shape in the air with her fingers. A high-pitched hum in her ears told her the wards were working.

She let out a breath and looked up. Topaz was settling in high above her.

"You really don't have to sleep up there," Mildred called.

"I'd rather not trust a witch," Topaz called back.

Mildred stared at the ground dismally. It looked hard and lumpy and uncomfortable. She'd never slept on dirt in her life.

A sliding, crashing sound made her look up.

"Here," Topaz said, dropping a pile of charms on her.

Mildred stared at them. "These are mine! When did you —?"

"While you were casting the spell."

"*Why?*"

Topaz grinned. "I'm very good at pickpocketing."

Mildred shoved the charms back in her pocket. "You're not the way I envisioned princesses," she muttered.

"Thank you." Topaz sounded pleased.

Mildred piled leaves under Topaz's tree and tried to curl up in a comfortable position. The ground felt hard-packed, and the stems were itchy, but she was exhausted enough from the stress of the day that her eyelids started to droop anyway.

"Topaz," she called up tiredly. "Are *you* trustworthy?"

"Nope!" Topaz called back, settling into her tree. "Thanks for asking!"

Chapter 16
Gingerbread

 thunderous snore made Mildred's eyes fly open.
She tensed, recognizing the forest scenery. *Where am I? Where —?*
Then she relaxed, remembering the wards she'd made. She thanked Witch Fyrailn silently and turned to go back to sleep.

SNORE!

Mildred sat bolt upright. She looked over and saw Topaz, now sprawled on the ground. Her mouth was open, and a leaf had fallen in it.

"You're *not* how I envisioned princesses," she muttered.

The humming in her ears fizzled, warning her the wards were dying. Mildred stretched, stumbled to her feet, and nudged the princess with her foot.

"Topaz," she whispered, "we need to get up."

The other girl didn't stir.

Mildred found a stick and poked her harder.

"Topaz," she repeated louder, "we need to get moving before the forest monsters find us."

The princess snored on.

Mildred frowned, tapping the stick against the ground. She drew in a large breath.

"TOPAZ!" she shouted, drawing in the air around her to magnify volume. "WAKE UP!"

Topaz sat bolt upright, her eyes huge.

Mildred panted for breath.

Topaz collapsed back onto the ground and started snoring again.

Mildred gritted her teeth and looked for a bigger stick.

Six minutes, two bellows, and eighteen more pokes later, Topaz swatted the stick away and muttered something unintelligible. By the time the princess staggered to her feet, it was over an hour later.

"Half a dozen dragons could have torched the forest, and you'd still be snoring right now!" Mildred shouted, throwing the stick to the ground.

"What do you mean, snoring?" Topaz mumbled, shoving a blanket back into her satchel. "I don't snore."

"Oh, yes you do."

"Princesses don't snore."

"They don't pick pockets, either."

"Obviously some do. And I don't snore." Topaz looked around with still-half-closed eyes. "Which way are we going?"

"Still think you shoulda waited till I was awake," Topaz mumbled, her eyes half-closed. "Been walking way too long. I bet that charm thing isn't working."

"It's working just fine," Mildred said testily. "I told it to take us to the edge of the forest. It can't possibly misinterpret that."

"Did you say *which* edge?" Topaz yawned.

Mildred froze.

"'Cause I'm sure there's one in every direction."

Mildred swallowed.

"We're lost," Topaz said flatly. "Aren't we."

"It depends on how you look at it," Mildred hedged.

Topaz opened her eyes blearily. "I'm looking. We're lost."

"Well, if you didn't sleep so deeply —!"

Topaz muttered something as she looked around them.

Mildred jerked the chain off her hand, feeling frustrated. That charm had willfully misunderstood her twice now. Granted, it had kept them away from monsters so far, which she'd also asked, but . . .

"That's made out of *food!*" Topaz cried, pointing.

Mildred spun around. Where there had just been trees a moment before, there was now a clearing with a cottage made out of gingerbread. It was trimmed with powdery frosting, and licorice twisted around the doorway.

"Want!" Topaz cried, looking greedy.

"No, you don't! A witch is bound to live there."

"Might not."

Two trees next to the cottage sprouted leaves that looked like cotton candy.

"Okay, probably," Topaz conceded.

Mildred brightened. "Wait a minute! We could ask for directions here!"

Topaz rubbed her eyes. "Directions from a witch. What a brilliant idea."

"Can you think of a better one?" Mildred retorted.

"Yes." Topaz pulled the satchel off her shoulder. "We stock up on gingerbread. I'm hungry."

Mildred marched towards the cottage. Rock candy cobblestones appeared under her feet.

"Hello?" she asked cautiously, knocking on the door.

Frosting oozed out of a shuttered window.

"We'd like to ask directions," Mildred went on politely.

Caramel apples swelled on the trees.

"Because we're lost, you see . . ."

Crack!

"Peppermint bark!" Topaz squealed.

The door blazed open, and a furious witch stood there. "Stop eating my house!" she bellowed.

"I'm not eating it," Topaz said, prying up a cobblestone. "I'm putting pieces in my bag for later. Why'd you make a house out of food if you don't want people doing that, anyway?"

"You eat my house, I eat *you!*" the witch snarled, waving her hand.

Mildred gaped. There was now a frog where Topaz had been standing.

"Better," the witch said. "Now for *you* . . ."

She jabbed her finger at Mildred. Nothing happened.

The hag frowned, looking at her finger. She pointed at Mildred again.

"I'm a witch, too," Mildred explained weakly. "Um . . . about those directions . . ."

The hag leaned forward, squinting. She peered at the badge on Mildred's cloak. "Black Magic Academy," she muttered. "Rotten school had the nerve to expel me. Had to finish off at Smoldering Institute."

"That's . . . that's where I'm headed next. Um . . . do you know where it is?"

"Sure." The hag pointed vaguely off to her left. "Somewhere out there."

"Um . . ." Mildred looked nervously behind her. "What about To— the pri— her? Did you mean what you said?"

"About what?"

"*'You eat my house . . .'*"

The hag smirked. "Maybe."

Mildred gulped.

"Though I usually just leave 'em frogs," the hag confided. "Done it to a duke's son last week. Bodyguards shoved me in my own fireplace, too. Good thing I'm a fire witch, eh?"

"Why *do* you live in a house made out of food if you don't want people eating it?" Mildred burst out.

"*I* eat it," the witch sniffed. "It's *mine*."

She reached out and snapped a caramel apple off the nearest tree. She bit into it, spraying juice everywhere.

"Brother enchanted the whole place," she mumbled through a mouthful. "Couldn' do it myself, of course. Not an earth witch."

"My Aunt Anklistine is," Mildred admitted. "But this isn't really her style, either."

"Anklistine?" The witch's eyes widened. She dropped the apple core, which liquified into lemonade. "Of Ebony Drake?"

Puzzled, Mildred nodded.

"Used to be friends with Hurda, didn't I? We even got expelled the same week!" The hag leaned forward eagerly. "They all still live there? Oplisa and Hurda and them?"

Mildred nodded.

"Ha!" The gingerbread witch clapped her hands. She looked gleeful. "Simply have to visit. But can't get in unless somebody invites me. Too many warding-spells. You live there?"

"W-well — I did. Before school."

"Should count. Invite me!"

Mildred just stared at her.

"I'll let you have the pest," the witch said slyly. "Even teach you how to make frogs yourself. What do you say?"

Mildred glanced back at Topaz, who was sitting on top of the satchel. She looked irritable and extremely warty.

"All right," Mildred said slowly.

"Come in, then!" The hag gestured eagerly. "Shouldn't take more than an hour or two!"

Swallowing, Mildred followed. *I know how to unravel any spell I can cast. I hope Topaz understands that. I hope she sees I'm not abandoning her.*

But that frog, sitting on the satchel, sure looked awfully lonely.

Chapter 17
Mirror, Mirror

Even though she was only gone half an hour, Mildred felt horribly guilty when she walked out and found the frog watching from a windowsill, looking accusing.

"I'm sorry," Mildred whispered, moving the princess to the ground.

The frog croaked huffily and hopped over to her satchel.

Mildred glanced back through the doorway, making sure the other witch was busy — she seemed to be packing and giggling — then quickly waved her hands to cast the unraveling.

Topaz mushroomed upwards again, ballooning into a human shape. The green, warty skin was the last thing to change, which made her look very odd indeed. Then red curls billowed outwards as Topaz snatched her gown from the dirt and shook it out in disgust.

"What's that I hear?" the gingerbread witch shouted from indoors. "Is somebody else out there?"

"No one!" Mildred called hastily. "I'm just — I'm just leaving. Have fun visiting Aunt Hurda!"

"Oh, yes," the witch cackled. "Fun, indeed!"

Mildred pushed the princess ahead of her as they hurried away from the clearing. As the cottage vanished, Topaz stopped to breathe and pull on underclothing.

"Gonna have to brush my hair out again," Topaz muttered, lacing up her corset. "Gets unmanageable quickly. And thanks."

Mildred swallowed. "I — I didn't get very useful directions. I'm sorry."

"'Sokay." Topaz grunted as she tied the laces. "Wasn't really worth the frog time, but at least we got snacks."

Startled, Mildred looked over at the satchel. Sure enough, it looked crammed full of rectangular things. "Are you sure that was wise?" she asked weakly.

"Nope," Topaz said, "but that's never stopped me."

Mildred rubbed her forehead as she watched the princess pull the silk gown over her head.

"Now," Topaz added, her voice muffled, "think you could take us to the nearest forest edge?"

Mildred hesitated. "It might be better to just ask to go to Smoldering Institute directly, since I'm already late. I could probably detour to find you the way out, though . . ."

"Nah." Topaz tied the bows on her sleeves and reached around to pull at her back-laces. "Those Institutes are fairly close to the capitol. Just a few days' journey. And I'm not really in a hurry."

Capitol. It was so strange to think that there were royalty who thought they ruled the kingdom.

"Besides," Topaz added, tugging a crease out of one sleeve, "once you're done there, you can come back with me and fix that dumb marquess. Since you can change frogs back, and all."

Startled, Mildred looked at her. She hadn't thought about that.

"Or better yet, teach Dorian," Topaz added brightly. "Then he could turn back the marquess *and* teach Chalk White a lesson!"

Mildred shuddered.

"Of course . . ." Topaz went on thoughtfully, "you'll probably want to steer clear of Father, either way. He's got that whole thing against magic. He's paranoid that someone's going to use it on him."

"Then why doesn't he just raid the Institutes?" Mildred burst out. "If they're so nearby, you'd think —"

Topaz grinned. "Oh, he's tried. But apparently you can't get in unless you're invited. Same with all witch schools, probably."

Is it really such a good idea to take her with me? Mildred wondered.

Topaz looped her arm through Mildred's. "Come on. Admit it. I'll make great company."

Mildred looked at the princess.

She certainly won't be boring, Mildred had to admit.

"All right," she said slowly.

Mildred twisted the charm around her wrist, trying in vain to find some way to hold it that didn't cut off her circulation.

Topaz yanked a brush through her wild curls, restraining several sections in small ribbons.

"Well?" the princess demanded, pointing at her hair.

Mildred glanced back, distracted. "Well what?"

"How do I look? Sufficiently courtly?"

"I wouldn't really know," Mildred admitted.

"Be that way," Topaz muttered. There was a rummaging sound, and Mildred glanced back to see her pulling out a large hand-mirror. "Mirror, mirror in my hand. Who's the most gorgeous princess in the land?"

"You are," it said in a tinny voice.

Mildred leapt backward. "It *talks?*" she squeaked.

"Yup! Dorian enchanted it for my last birthday. Said it's because I'm so terribly vain."

"Does it actually scour the land to judge?" Mildred asked, awed. That sounded like an incredibly difficult talisman to make.

"Nah. It's just empty flattery." Topaz grinned. "But that's why I like it. It's funny!"

Mildred frowned. She didn't really see why that was funny.

"Of course, my best friend's stepdaughter has no sense of humor," Topaz added, sniffing. "So the brat got terribly offended when she caught us playing with it."

"Your . . . best friend has a stepdaughter?"

"Yup. Lily. Though everybody calls her Chalk White because she claims the sun would spoil her 'perfect complexion.'"

"How old is she?" Mildred asked, astonished.

"Chalk White? Seventeen."

"I mean your best friend."

"Oh, Ranestia? She's sixteen."

Mildred stared at her in horror.

"Political arrangement," Topaz shrugged. "You know how it is."

"How could she agree to that?" Mildred squeaked. "Her husband must have been twenty years older than her!"

"Forty. And she wasn't given a choice. Besides, it worked out fine; he died of overeating last year, and she inherited everything. Met Dorian at the funeral, actually. That's her boyfriend."

Mildred stared at her.

"Of course, nothing's perfect," Topaz sighed. "Chalk White *does* keep trying to kill her. But Ranestia's got seven bodyguards, which usually does the trick."

"That's the most horrible thing I've ever heard!" Mildred cried.

Topaz gave her a puzzled look. "Why? That's how marriage works in the aristocracy. Anyway, my father's far more reasonable than Ranestia's dad — it's unlikely he'll choose someone I hate."

"What if he does?" Mildred challenged.

Topaz grinned. "Then I'll drive the guy off with my personality."

"I've always thought marriage should be about love," Mildred muttered.

"*Love?*" Topaz stared at her incredulously. "That just opens you to heartbreak and humiliation. No, thanks. Much better to be practical about things."

Mildred stared at her. *You must be insane.*

"And speaking of practical," Topaz added, slowing down, "are you sure we're not going by a lair of manticores or something?"

"I asked the charm to keep us away from all monsters."

Topaz stopped. "Uh . . . no you didn't."

"Yes, I did."

"Are you *sure?*"

"Of course I'm sure!"

"Then why don't I remember you saying it?"

Mildred hesitated, looking down at the chain. She *had* asked that part, hadn't she? Surely she wouldn't have forgotten something so important.

"Why do you ask?" she asked slowly.

"Because there are no birds singing." Topaz gestured at the trees around them. "Doesn't strike me as a good thing."

Mildred swallowed.

"Can you cast wards behind us?" Topaz demanded.

"Not ones that follow," Mildred muttered, her face flushing.

Topaz sighed. "Of course not. That would be too useful."

"Those are tenth-level!" Mildred protested. "I haven't even gotten into Summoning Elements!"

"Mildred," Topaz said through clenched teeth, "I can *see* a cerberus behind us."

Sweating, Mildred started pinching the air and murmuring.

"Mildred," Topaz snarled, "cast — wards — *now!*"

Mildred turned and flung her arm backwards. The cerberus leapt. *Crash!*

Furious, the cerberus picked itself off the ground and started howling.

"It's got a pack!" Topaz groaned. "Run!"

Mildred broke into a terrified sprint.

Answering howls echoed in front of them. Mildred glanced off to the side and saw a three-headed puppy veering towards them.

"*Topaz!*" she screamed.

"Cast wards on the side, too!" Topaz shouted back.

"I *can't!* Not without releasing —"

THUMP.

Mildred stopped abruptly, her jaw gaping. Where the massive puppy had been, there was now a huge mound of dirt.

"Wh-what?" Mildred sputtered. "Did you do that?"

"Do I *look* like a witch?" Topaz shot back, gasping for breath.

"Phooey," a voice grumbled behind them.

They spun around. An ugly man with beard stubble was rubbing his hands through his unwashed hair.

"I thought you were my little sister," he complained. "I don't suppose you've seen another wind witch around here anywhere? Overweight, probably in a bad mood, named Trasia?"

Chapter 18
Smoldering Institute

isbelieving, Mildred stared at him.

"No idea who that is," Topaz said.

"*Trasia?*" Mildred gaped. "You know *Trasia?*"

"Then you've seen her!" The man brightened. "Which way did she go?"

Mildred stared at him, thunderstruck. "I — I haven't seen her. It's just — we were friends at the Academy. Before she got expelled."

"Oh, worst day of my life," the man muttered. "Put back in charge of my slacker little sister. Her and mom fighting all the time. Now she says she wants to go to Cyclone Institute. Like they would accept her after she failed everything?"

"It wasn't her fault she flunked," Mildred protested, stung. "She's a village witch, so everybody —"

"Mom got through just fine," the man retorted, scratching his chin. "And our great-aunt was third-best in her year."

"It's still not her fault," Mildred said heatedly.

"Wait a minute," Topaz interrupted. "You. What's your name?"

"Aethan."

"Topaz. You say you're going to Cyclone Institute?"

"Assuming she's not lost around here, I suppose I'll have to," Aethan said grumpily.

"Great!" Topaz beamed. "You can show us the way. Mildred's headed for Smoldering."

Aethan eyed Mildred. "You're not a fire witch."

"It's an errand," Topaz explained. "What do you say? Could you?"

"Guess so," Aethan muttered. "Been this way a dozen times while I was going to Hemlock. But I don't really want to."

"Too bad!" Topaz clapped her hands. "Lead the way!"

Aethan just stared at her.

"*Topaz.* Remember the name? I'm your princess. I command you."

Aethan rolled his eyes and started walking.

Other than warding off a swarm of vampire wasps and trapping three giant spiders, Aethan spent the rest of the journey ignoring them. This didn't stop Topaz from chattering incessantly in his direction, however. At last, as the sky was darkening and the trees were thinning, they reached the edge of a cliff.

"Stop," Aethan directed. "Don't fall. Do you see?"

Topaz shielded her eyes and squinted. "Nope. Nothing."

An explosion hovered in the valley far beneath them, frozen mid-flame. Smoke coiled around it, drifting lazily but never dissipating.

"That's Smoldering Institute?" Mildred whispered.

"What is?" Topaz asked, craning.

"That's where it's supposed to be," Aethan shrugged. "I've never seen it."

A tongue of flame spat out and sizzled past Mildred. It hit the dirt, then broiled up into a plasma bridge.

Mildred glanced back at Aethan.

"Go in?" he suggested.

"Let me go with you!" Topaz cried, grabbing Mildred's arm. "They really should let me in! Dad technically owns all land in this country —"

Aethan snorted with amusement.

"Is something wrong?" Topaz asked, irritated.

"Nope. Feel free to try it. Love to see you fall to your death."

Topaz glared at him.

Nervously, Mildred placed a toe on the bridge. It seemed solid enough. She moved onto it slowly with her whole foot. The glittering spikes held.

"If that's a bridge, I wouldn't trust it to last forever," Aethan yawned. "Try not to linger."

Swallowing, Mildred put another foot on the bridge and took a step forward. Then another. Then another.

"Promise you'll come to visit!" Topaz cried. "Promise you'll come change the frog back for me!"

I can't promise, Mildred thought. But she looked back at them.

"Thank you," she called.

"Yeah," Aethan muttered. "Whatever."

Smoke flickered past and obscured her vision. Then it moved past, and the cliffside was gone. There was only endless bridge behind, and forward into the flame.

Sweating as she walked through the heat, Mildred realized that the tongues of flame ahead had licked into a building. It was impossibly tall and skinny and glittered like a fractured beetle, each facet gleaming with a flickering light.

The closer she crept, the worse her head ached, and the more transfixed she became by the building. What she'd taken for flickering now appeared to be living flames, trapped inside the walls or perhaps leaping through them. When she took her final wobbly step off of the bridge, she collapsed by the entrance, looking up hopefully.

There was no doorway.

"Help!" Mildred croaked. Her throat felt raw and dry. "Help! Somebody! I'm here from Black Magic Academy. High Witch Tractia sent me. I'm not a fire witch! Please let me in!"

The wall ahead of her shattered.

A woman stepped through the inferno, wearing robes made of living flame.

"Wind witch," she murmured through pursed lips. Her skin looked sunburned, and her eyes were crimson. "What an insult. Tractia failed to mention that."

"Are you — a teacher here?" Mildred asked faintly.

"Kantaro," the woman said tightly. "I'm the High Witch."

Mildred stared at her, swaying. Her mind felt fuzzy.

"Come in," High Witch Kantaro snapped, smashing her hand through the wall. "Tomorrow will be a busy day."

Mildred followed her into the building, licking her dry lips. When a blast of mere uncomfortable warmth hit her face, it felt blissful, like a cool breeze.

"Water," the High Witch murmured, pointing at an indoor fountain. "You probably need it."

Thankfully, Mildred dove for one of the goblets that lined the floor and downed about eight cupfuls before she felt better. By the time she finished, she felt sluggish and sloshy.

"*Wind*," the High Witch muttered, smashing through another wall to lead her to a spiral staircase. "What was she thinking?"

Mildred stumbled up the staircase, following in a haze of exhaustion. The staircase seemed to go on forever, endlessly, interminably. It looked large enough to fit three people side-by-side, yet they met no one else going up or down it, and there seemed to be no doorways, no floors, nothing but this endless spiral staircase with its smooth, flickering walls on every side.

"Need sleep," Mildred gasped finally, collapsing on a stair and fighting to keep from crying.

The High Witch of Smoldering Institute paused.

"The lower rooms belong to those of inferior physical strength," she said archly. "They are considered a disgrace."

"Don't care." Mildred buried her head in her arms, almost slurring the words. "Need *sleep*."

There was silence a long moment. Then a shattering sound. Mildred looked up blearily to find shards of wall scattered around her.

"Sleep, then," High Witch Kantaro said sharply. "Shame on Tractia for not implementing strict exercise regimes."

Mildred stumbled into the tiny room, which was shaped like an eighth of a circle. It held no furniture except a pile of cushions in the sharpest corner, and she stumbled towards those gratefully. As the wall slurped closed behind her, she plummeted, closing her eyes.

She wished someone would turn off the lights in this horrible place.

Chapter 19
Into the Fire

"I heard a rumor," a furious voice said. "But of course I dismissed it as nonsense."

Mildred's eyes cracked open. She was still tired. The cloak hood had twisted around her face.

"I mean, who *walks* to their death?" the voice went on, snarling. "Who would be that *stupid?* Why, nobody! At least, that's what you'd think."

Mildred forced herself to stand and twisted the hood around. She squinted through the bright light. "Rulisa?"

"You had *escaped!*" Rulisa screamed. "You were *free!* Why did you come? *Why?* Were you completely *insane?*"

"What're you doing here?" Mildred mumbled, rubbed her eyes. "Did you defect?"

"I'm here for the same reason you are!"

Mildred rubbed her shoulders, which felt stiff. She tried to think. Her thoughts felt sluggish. "I'm not sure High Witch Tractia ever explained it."

"Of course she didn't," Rulisa fumed.

Mildred swallowed, dropping her arms. She was starting to feel more awake now. "What am I supposed to do?" she asked trepidatiously.

"The same thing I am!" Rulisa exploded. "It's obvious!"

Mildred stared at her.

"Did she send you to deliver a message, too?" Rulisa growled.

"To a giant?" Mildred asked slowly.

"Mine was an ogre."

Mildred shivered.

"Not that ogres can read," Rulisa muttered, "which was her miscalculation. Just because the species was made out of humans doesn't mean they're intelligent. The original people were all stupid, illiterate thugs. That hasn't changed."

"Ogres were made out of humans?"

"Giants, too. And goblins. We learned how in History of Metamorphosis."

Mildred tried to wrap her mind around this. Even Drakin wouldn't have had the power to do something that extreme.

"So, the ogre opened the message and made me read it out loud to him." Rulisa's ears turned red. "It was an invitation to eat me! He howled with laughter, the creep. So I turned him into an ant."

Mildred's eyes widened.

"I did make him a cat later," Rulisa muttered gracelessly. "Gave him to some miller's family to raise. But I was this close to squashing the ant."

Mildred sat down on the cushions, feeling wobbly. Had the letter she'd delivered to the giantess said something similar?

"But then!" Rulisa screamed. "*Then* High Witch Tractia had the nerve to congratulate me and order me here! And all she'd say about it was some stupid excuse about spy-spells that any Fifth Class student would know couldn't work!"

Mildred swallowed. They would?

"So of course it was obvious," Rulisa said grimly. "I checked, and sure enough, you'd been sent here, too."

"I still don't . . ." Mildred said slowly.

"Killing's forbidden on Academy grounds."

Mildred stared at her.

"Whereas here, death-matches are considered sport."

"What?" Mildred gasped. "But —"

"But what?" Rulisa asked nastily. "Students aren't supposed to hold them? Death-matches should be voluntary? This isn't a fair battlefield? Believe me, I've tried those already."

"But why would High Witch Tractia want either of us *dead?* We're both valuable students!"

Rulisa stared at her with pursed lips. Then she marched over and snatched the badge off Mildred's cloak.

"That's why."

"Give it back!" Mildred cried.

"*Give it back?* I shouldn't have been able to take it from you in the first place."

Mildred grabbed the badge and slapped it back on her cloak.

It fell off.

Startled, Mildred picked it up again.

"You're *expelled,* you numbskull!" Rulisa exploded. "As soon as the High Witch thought you had run away!"

Mildred gaped at her. "But I didn't — why would she —"

"*Why?*" Rulisa asked incredulously. "You've made practically no effort to hide how meek you are. Not to mention that nonsense with defending me! I tried to warn you, but you wouldn't listen. White magic is anathema to our school, and High Witch Tractia is not stupid."

"Well, what about you?" Mildred whispered. "You're no more evil than I am. She must suspect you, too."

"Impossible," Rulisa said flatly.

"Why?" Mildred demanded.

"Three reasons." Rulisa's ears darkened. "First, I am significantly better at, as you once put it, *lying.* Second, Kraken Institute also permits death-matches. If she wanted us to be on equal footing, she would have sent us there. And, finally . . ."

Rulisa's face twisted.

"Finally, if she wanted me dead, she wouldn't have needed to make up an elaborate excuse. You're Drakin's daughter. Oplisa's niece. My mother's name carries significantly less weight."

Mildred swallowed.

"And of course I'll win," Rulisa said bitterly. "You're under-educated. You're not as powerful. Not to mention that you have the fighting spirit of a doormat."

"Now, wait a minute!" Mildred said heatedly.

"But I don't want to kill anyone," Rulisa muttered. "Not even you."

"You don't have to!" Mildred cried. "You're a fire witch — just blast open a wall and let me escape!"

"Not happening."

"Why not?" Mildred protested. "If you really want to save me —"

"I don't want to save you," Rulisa growled. "I just don't want to kill you."

She smashed her fist into a wall and stormed out. The hole slurped closed before Mildred could reach it. She clawed until her nails were sore and pounded her arms on it in frustration.

I hate this building, she thought miserably.

High Witch Kantaro smashed a hole in the wall.

"Mildrin?" she asked in a sickly-sweet voice. "Everyone's waiting for you!"

Mildred gulped and went on holding her breath. She'd never mastered invisibility, but wind witches were supposed to have an advantage with it . . .

High Witch Kantaro sighed. "Oh, well. Be difficult." She snapped her fingers, and jets of fire blazed from the ceiling.

Mildred yelped and dove for the doorway. A strong hand snatched her wrist before she was through.

"It's much too late to cower out now." Sunlight blazed through the outer walls, speckling rainbows across High Witch Kantaro's face. "So don't struggle. It'll only weaken you before the competition, and we'd prefer a decent show."

Mildred fought, but High Witch Kantaro never released her iron grip. In what seemed like no time, she was dragged up to the sweltering heights of the building.

"This is not fair!" Mildred wailed. "Nothing about this is voluntary!"

Smirking, High Witch Kantaro smashed the ceiling over their heads and shoved her through it.

The floor sizzled shut, and Mildred gasped as the heat intensified. The musty air clung to her lungs, and the stench of cinders was overpowering. The tip of the conical ceiling blazed white-hot, and the single spiral ledge running from floor to ceiling seemed crammed with every single student or teacher.

Halfway hidden underneath the highest end of the ledge was Rulisa. Her face was shadowed, but black smoke coiled around her ears. She did not look happy to be here.

"Welcome, students!" High Witch Kantaro called, waving her hands. "Who wants to cheer the wind witch?"

One or two halfhearted cheers.

"Who wants to cheer the fire witch?"

The bulk of the students roared.

"Begin!" High Witch Kantaro shouted.

Rulisa stepped forward into the light, her jaw set grimly. She unwound a single long black hair from her wrist. Giving it a sharp shake, she lashed it out like a whip.

Mildred dove to the side, her arm suddenly stinging as the whip hit. She yanked out her pockets, seizing a doughy ball.

There!

The tension charm smacked Rulisa in the face. She stiffened. Then she clamped her fingers around the ball, and white ashes fluttered away.

Mildred stared at her, stunned. *Why didn't that work?*

Rulisa cracked the whip, which sizzled. Sparks crackled down its length and arced at the tip. She snapped it back at Mildred again.

Mildred barely managed to dodge, her mind working feverishly.

Of course. There were no air currents to work with.

Wind magic was barely worth anything here.

Worst battleground ever!

Rulisa spun the whip forward. It missed Mildred and scraped the wall instead.

Think! Mildred thought frantically. *Think! Think!*

A whispery crystalline sound made her jerk her head back, and she realized it came from the wall behind her. It was healing up the tiniest splintered cracks.

The whip. Mildred's eyes widened. *Of course.*

She waited until Rulisa paced nearer, her eyes narrowed in fierce concentration. She reached into her pocket and looped her fingers around the tangle of ribbon and string. Her nails tingled as she activated it.

Rulisa raised her arm, whip coiling —

Mildred flung the darkness charm at her.

Billows of black poured out across the room. Several students gasped. In the seconds of panicked confusion, Mildred snatched the whip and hurled it against the wall.

Crash!

Fresh air! She dove towards it, lurched through, and then felt herself plummeting.

Heights! Mildred screamed silently. She closed her eyes, reached out, and tried to seize one of the currents her fall was creating.

Wind. Wind. Wind. Wind. *I can't fly, but I can glide. If I just concentrate, I might be able to slow my fall just enough —*

SLAM.

Mildred choked and coughed as she found herself doubled across the thin handle of a wooden broomstick.

"Naughty, naughty," a male teacher said slyly. "You're not the first student to try that sort of thing. But believe me, there's no escape."

He zoomed to the top of the building and blasted a hole through the wall. His muscular arms shot her through it.

She rolled to Rulisa's feet.

Silence stretched across the room as the spectators leaned forward. The air sizzled with anticipation.

"I tried to escape," Mildred whispered. "It didn't work."

"Shut up," Rulisa hissed.

"You're going to have to make a decision."

"Shut up."

"Look around. They're just like Vaysa."

"Shut up."

"You really want to impress people like *this?*"

"*SHUT — UP!*"

Flames blazed up from Rulisa's ears and roared down her hair. Feathers exploded all over her body. The ceiling erupted in molten plasma. Students panicked and screamed.

With an unearthly shriek, a sharp pair of talons seized Mildred. She felt herself wrenched up, up, up, far into the sky.

Mildred fainted.

Chapter 20
Capitol

PLASH!

Mildred broke to the surface of a large lake, gasping. She looked around, realized Rulisa was gone, and shot an air bubble downwards. Her head felt amazingly clear. She felt better, smarter, and more healthy than she had in ages.

Rulisa broke to the surface, gasping. Her arms were covered in tattered brown feathers, now waterlogged and wilting. "Can't — swim —" she choked.

Mildred blew a cushion of air underneath her. Rulisa doubled over, coughing, and the feathers sparked and sizzled away.

"I knew you weren't a nightbat."

"*Stupid — talisman!*" Rulisa snarled. "*Stupid — phoenix!*"

"Healing fire," Mildred said quietly, noticing that even her scrapes and bruises were gone. "You're a natural at it."

"Mom wouldn't have touched the magic," Rulisa muttered miserably.

"How did you plan to pass Familiar Talismans pretending to be a *nightbat?* At least karkadanns and unicorns look similar!"

"I hate you," Rulisa sobbed. "They're going to expel me. Everybody knows now. It's all your fault!"

"You could never have gotten away with it," Mildred offered, trying to sound sensible. "Even if you made it up to thirteenth-level Talismans, they would have caught you then. Isn't it better to have that happen now, when you're far away?"

"*Hate* you," Rulisa sobbed. "I would have done it somehow."

Witch Fyrailn usually teaches all the thirteenth-level classes, Mildred thought. *There's no way something that obvious would sneak by her.*

But she didn't say it. It would just sound churlish.

"I don't have anywhere to go!" Mildred cried, suddenly realizing. "I don't have *anyone* who'd take me!"

"Well, you're not welcome here," Rulisa growled, jabbing her thumb off to the side. "Dad would hate you just as much as I do."

Mildred followed her gaze to a large, tidy-looking house made out of dark wood. Halfway hidden between thornbushes, it looked haughty, aloof, but not actually menacing. She stared at it as her bubble drifted them nearer to the shore.

Dad, Mildred thought slowly. The word penetrated.

"Do you know where my father is?" she whispered, squeezing her sodden sleeves. "Do you know where I could find him?"

Rulisa's eyes darkened. Her hair began to wisp steam.

"I don't know anything about him," Mildred pleaded. "Only his name. Which you told me. If you could just say where he is —"

The water around Rulisa boiled. "Find him yourself. I'll have nothing to do with it."

She plunged her feet downward, seemed to catch dirt, and sloshed towards the shore.

"Wait!" Mildred cried. "Are you sure we can't be friends?"

Rulisa spun around, her ears blazing. "Don't ever let me see you again," she snarled. "You've cost me my dream!"

"*You!*" the princess squealed. "You *are* coming home with me! I knew I could talk you into it!"

Mildred smiled weakly, holding up the directional charm. "It actually worked properly this time."

"Yay!" Topaz clapped her hands. "Now we can turn back the frog, and everything! How long before you have to go back to school?"

"I — I — I can't go back." Mildred hunched her shoulders, ashamed. "I can't even go home again. If I did, my aunts would . . . well . . . I think things would end badly."

Topaz's eyes widened. "You mean you're a fugitive?"

Mildred ducked her head. She nodded jerkily.

"Perfect!" Topaz squealed. "I've always wanted to harbor fugitives!"

"I . . . I just found out yesterday," Mildred mumbled. "And I thought . . . well . . . maybe . . . you could help me find my father? He wasn't a witch, you see. Maybe . . . he . . ."

"Oh. Sure." Topaz looked bored. "We probably have records and things. But in the meantime, let's hear about what went wrong! That sounds exciting!"

Mildred swallowed and started explaining.

". . . And that's why Dad hates witches," Topaz finished, taking a breath. "He really, really hates it when people remind him that his hair's still bright blue, which is why I nicknamed him King Bluebeard. What's wrong?"

Mildred just stood there, frozen with terror.

"What's wrong?" Topaz repeated.

"How many people are here?" Mildred asked hoarsely, pointing with a shaking finger at the crowd of people screaming and running and shoving one another just past the city gates.

"Oh, maybe a hundred thousand," Topaz shrugged. "Not sure. It fluctuates."

A hundred thousand. Mildred could barely process such a figure. She just stood there, stunned and overwhelmed.

"Merchants," Topaz said, jabbing her finger towards stalls of shouting people. "Houses," she went on, pointing at shabby wooden buildings behind them. "Sheep," she added, wrinkling her nose as a flock of woolly clamor neared them. "Disgusting things."

"These are all — Normals?" Mildred asked hoarsely.

"Might be a few witches. But almost all, probably."

Mildred stared around her numbly. *So this is a city. This is how most Normal aristocracy lives.*

Above her, someone poured out something horrible into a gutter.

It splashed, rebounded, and the smell wafted past.

Mildred flinched. *And it reeks.*

Drawing nearer to the center of the city, the stench was masked by gaggingly strong perfume, while merchants now seemed to offer far more upscale things. The few people lining these streets were dressed opulently, and the gutters were replaced by thick tubes. Everything looked rich and well-kept.

"YOU!" A man in uniform charged at them. "You — you — you've been missing ten days!"

"Oh, hi, Lanon," Topaz said in a bored voice. "Mildred, this is one of my bodyguards. He hates it when I give him the slip."

"Do you want me to get fired?" the man shouted. "Or executed?"

"That wouldn't happen unless I die," Topaz snorted. "Don't exaggerate, honestly."

"I'm taking you back to the castle *right now!*"

Topaz eyed him speculatively. "Out of curiosity, how much would it cost to keep you silent for another hour about seeing me?"

"You can't buy me!" the man howled. "Of all the insulting —!"

Topaz wrenched a sash from her dress. It ripped, and a fat gold disc fell into her hand.

"This work?" she asked.

The man stopped, his eyes widening.

Topaz held it up, the afternoon sun glinting off a bearded face.

"Half an hour," he said.

"Four hours."

"Three hours. And you make sure someone else is on duty next time you run away."

"Deal." Topaz plonked the disc in his hand.

The guard seized it and ran for a building that smelled strongly of rotten grapes.

Topaz smirked. "That'll keep him busy for the rest of the day."

"What was that disc?" Mildred asked curiously.

Topaz gave her a strange stare. "You mean the coin?"

"That round thing."

"How can you possibly not know about money?!"

Mildred just stared at her.

"People use money to buy things," Topaz explained. "It's like barter, only everybody wants these."

"Barter?" Mildred repeated, slowly. She'd never heard of that, either.

"Your family *does* trade for things, don't they?"

"Um," Mildred admitted, chewing her lip. "Not really. What they can't make, they just sort of take."

Topaz groaned. "This explains why you didn't recognize me — I'm on the penny. See?" She pulled a tiny, tarnished disc out of her pocket and held it out.

Mildred stared at it for a moment. It held the picture of a five-year-old girl who looked sweet and innocent and nothing like Topaz.

"Um . . ."

"All right, so they haven't updated my picture for awhile," Topaz said testily.

Topaz bribed two more guards at the castle's front gate, so they let her and Mildred in without comment.

"How do you convince them to let you leave?" Mildred whispered, watching the guards crank thick metal chains to pull the stone doors open. It took awhile.

"I don't," Topaz whispered back. "There's a secret passage Great-Grandfather built to escape the castle in case of siege. He was kind of a tyrant, so he had reason to worry. It only works one-way, though."

The doors rolled open, revealing a cavernous entryway. Stone pillars ran from floor to ceiling, brash and intimidating. But, bizarrely, someone had crisscrossed ribbons around the pillars, and a patchwork of colorful carpets coated the floor.

"Fabian's redecorated," Topaz said knowingly.

Spotting a gaggle of maids, Topaz shoved Mildred up a staircase covered in tiny gold knots, then through a huge empty room lit with iron chandeliers. When they reached a hallway marbled in surreal white and grey, Mildred began to get a headache.

"Why doesn't anything match?" she complained.

"Eighty-six different court artists," Topaz shrugged. "Judging by the entrance, Fabian's in favor this week."

Ducking to avoid a manservant, the princess pushed her into a well-polished conference room — everything dark wood or covered in hand-spun lace — then out a different door and down another hallway, this one draped in billowing silk curtains.

They turned a corner and found everything covered in tapestry.

"I see Aunt Arabel bribed someone again," Topaz sneered.

Looking closely, Mildred noticed all of them looked sloppily stitched. Among the worst was the largest, which featured a simpering ten-year-old girl. Threads were missing, colors mismatched, and the whole composition looked garish.

"Don't ask," Topaz said darkly. "Just don't. She made me pose for that thing for weeks."

The next section of hallway plunged them into darkness. Wind whistled eerily in the dark, then the ceiling blazed in irregular patterns. Blinded, Mildred flinched away — only to discover that the wall beside her was now covered in gory battle scenes.

"Dad's third wife hired this artist," Topaz muttered. "I wish we'd get rid of him already."

Mildred breathed a sigh of relief as they turned a corner and passed through an open, well-lit space.

"This way," Topaz called, lifting the latch to a jeweled door.

Mildred hurried after her into a large central room. It held several bright couches, and three doorways branched away. One displayed a small bedroom covered in brocade. One seemed to be a place for bathing. The largest was filled with tall, wooden wardrobes.

A maid exited the bathroom and dropped her change of linens.

"Your highness!" she gasped. "You're back already!"

"And before anyone saw me," Topaz smirked, flopping onto a jewel-toned couch with satisfaction. "Life is good."

"If — your highness – will excuse me —"

The maid backed out of the room.

"Wait!" Topaz sat bolt upright. "I order you to not tell anybody."

The maid stared at her with panicked eyes.

"Because I want to change my clothes," Topaz sniffed. "You don't want Father walking in while I'm bathing, do you?"

The maid turned red and ran out.

"That should buy us some time," Topaz said, stretching. "You need to get rid of that black thing. It looks witchy, not to mention just plain ugly. This way."

Mildred followed her into the largest room, stomach coiling. Topaz threw open several wardrobes, revealing a stunning array of bright colors.

"Pick one," she gestured. "I've got more."

Overwhelmed, Mildred ran her fingers along several of the nearest dresses. They were all light fabric, soft despite their sleekness, and beautiful. Just the sort of thing Aunt Oplisa would never get her. She pulled out one of pale blue and held it out mutely.

Topaz cocked her head to the side. "All right," she said. "Pastels might look good on you."

She helped Mildred lace up the back with practiced efficiency. Then she wrinkled her nose, looking down at her feet. "Those have *got* to go."

She flung open another wardrobe and scanned through shelf after shelf of shoes. Finally, she reached for a pair of blue velvet boots.

"Off with the slippers," she ordered, gesturing. "Off, off."

Mildred swallowed and obeyed.

Topaz shoved the boots on her. Then frowned.

"Your feet are tiny. Maybe Mom's old shoes will fit you."

She strode to a corner wardrobe, stood on tiptoes to open the top cabinet, then pulled down an array of glass slippers. She wrinkled her nose as she tried one of them up to Mildred's feet.

"Almost. It's not fair. I had to take after Father with these boatlike things."

In the end, she unearthed a pair of smallish purple slippers and winched ribbons around the edges. Then she flung open another wardrobe, which revealed an enormous full-length mirror.

"Gosh, my hair needs brushing again," Topaz squinted. "And so does yours. Brush." She tossed Mildred a jewel-encrusted hairbrush. "Use it."

Topaz swept her own hairbrush through her curls. She preened for several minutes, scrutinizing her reflection. Then she squinted back at

Mildred, whose shoulder-length hair hadn't taken long to tidy.

"Better," the princess muttered. "But way too short."

Mildred touched her thin hair uncomfortably.

"We could braid it. No, wait — ponytail. Or pigtails."

Mildred stared at her in horror.

Topaz grinned. "Pigtails it is!"

Mildred struggled, but the princess held her still with iron determination. In no time, her hair was pulled up in two bunches with silk flowers twisted in them. Mildred stared at herself in the mirror, confounded. She looked like some noble's daughter.

Like my father's daughter? she wondered, swallowing.

Loud trumpets sounded in the hallway.

"Ooh!" Topaz's face lit up. "Come on, come on, hurry!"

She raced through the doorway, tugging Mildred with her. She threw Mildred on the couch and flung herself down, red curls bouncing. Then she faced the door eagerly.

Another two trumpets sounded. An enormous red-faced, blue-bearded man smashed the door open and stormed through it.

"*TOPAZ SARDION ANGELICA RENTAV!*" he bellowed.

Mildred cringed.

Topaz smiled and smoothed out her skirt.

"Hi, Daddy," she beamed.

Chapter 21
King Bluebeard

ing Bluebeard loomed over them. He looked every inch a man who would execute someone in his rage.

"*You ran away again!*" he shouted. "*AGAIN! WITHOUT PERMISSION!*"

"Yes, that's usually what 'running away' means."

"*THIS HAS GOT TO STOP!*"

"Since when?"

"Since I *SAID SO!*"

Topaz yawned. "Oh, well, if that's the reason . . ."

"You're practically adult! You're marriageable age! Why can't you *behave?*"

"Because it's boring. And one of my governesses keeps trying to convince me to pick up needlework. *Needlework.* How is that supposed to help me run the country?"

"I'M JUST TRYING TO TEACH YOU MANNNERS!"

"YOU COULD START BY USING A FEW ON ME!"

"Stop it!" Mildred shouted, leaping up. "Stop yelling at each other! Why can't you just — why can't — why can't you just get *along?*"

The king and princess stared at her.

"This is getting along," Topaz said, sounding puzzled. "You should see us on a bad day."

"Didn't notice you had company," King Bluebeard rumbled.

"I could send her out," Topaz offered.

"No. Not worth the effort," the king muttered. "We'll discuss this later."

Two trumpets sounded outside the door as the king grouched out of the room.

Topaz sighed and stretched. "Great. Now he's going to ignore me for days. I only ever get attention when he's angry at me."

"That's really your father?" Mildred asked in disbelief. "He's just so — so — so —"

"Ugly?" Topaz grinned. "I know. I take after my mom. He held a ball to find someone beautiful — he said the royal family had too much ugly already — and she won. She didn't mention that she'd stolen her clothes and jewelry, or that she was a palace servant, until after the wedding." Topaz smirked. "Too bad she died so young. I bet I would have liked her."

"I never knew my mother either, but I doubt I would have liked her," Mildred muttered. "Of course, my aunts are always going on about how perfect she was."

"Oh, mine too!" Topaz cried. "Mom's stepsisters are totally odious."

"I bet I had it worse!" Mildred laughed. "I have an aunt who only ever calls me 'Drakin's daughter.'"

"Oh, yeah? I have a grandmother who only ever calls *me* 'Thurgold's daughter.'"

"Ha! I bet you've never seen anyone half as ugly as Aunt Hur—" Mildred choked.

"What?" Topaz asked. "What's wrong?"

"*What* did you just call your father?" Mildred squeaked.

"His name."

"Which is *what?*"

"You really ought to know the name of your own king," Topaz said, exasperated.

"You called him *Thurgold!*"

"Yeah, but I prefer 'King Bluebeard.'"

"I need to go," Mildred burst out, scrambling to her feet.

"Why?" Topaz demanded. "What's the big deal?"

Mildred shook her head and tore the ribbons off her slippers. Her hands were shaking.

"Hang on," Topaz said slowly. "Did you say 'Drakin'?"

Mildred ran for her cloak.

Topaz dogged her heels.

"Because, you know — ha ha — that was Dad's third wife's name."

Mildred threw it on and fumbled to fasten it.

Topaz seized her wrists. "Why are you running away?"

Mildred swallowed. She couldn't face her.

Topaz's grip tightened. "Are you my sister?" she demanded.

Mildred shook her head quickly.

"You look like Drakin," Topaz said, her grip tightening. "I never thought to look for it before, but you do."

Mildred blinked back tears. She'd never hated her mother more.

Topaz let go, rubbing her head. "I don't believe I'm thinking this," she muttered. "It's impossible."

Mildred ran for the door.

"WAIT!" Topaz commanded.

Mildred halted halfway through the doorway.

"Impossible or not," Topaz said slowly, "we have to ask Dad."

Mildred shook her head, panicking.

"Do you really not want to know?" Topaz asked sharply. "Where else could you go, anyway?"

Tears pricked the corners of Mildred's eyes. She'd forgotten about that.

"It'll be fine," Topaz said, putting an arm around her shoulders. "You just have to know how to talk to him."

"*Dad!*" Topaz bellowed, pounding on the door. "Open up before I use my lockpicks!"

The door smashed open.

"*Lockpicks?*" the king roared. "You are not supposed to have *lockpicks!* If I find the man who sold them to you —"

"Dad," Topaz said, pointing at Mildred, "this is Drakin's daughter. Might be yours, too."

The king froze.

"What?" he rasped.

"Draaaaakin," Topaz repeated, as if he were an idiot. "Your third wife.

The one you always insisted wasn't a witch."

The king yanked them both into the room and slammed the door, breathing heavily.

"What do you mean, Drakin's daughter?" he snarled.

"I mean 'Drakin's daughter,'" Topaz shot back. "A person who is, incidentally, a witch. So, you total liar, it was *not* just my imagination, was it?"

The king's face flamed. "You were three. Far too young to know that —"

"That my life was in *danger?* Because my stepmother *enchanted* people? Thank you so much! I feel so safe!"

"This . . . this thing can't be my daughter," King Thurgold growled, jabbing his finger at Mildred. "If Drakin had been pregnant, I would have seen."

"B-but —" Mildred began.

"Hello! Illusion!" Topaz called. "Ever hear of it?"

My king's face paled. His beard look even bluer.

"Impossible," he whispered.

Topaz exhaled. "Yeah. But we could find out. I'm sure we could find a witch in Byrin who could —"

"Absolutely not," the king growled. "There will be no magic in my household. Never magic in my household."

"Then what are you planning to do?" Topaz demanded. "Accept an imposter? Or ignore a true daughter?"

The king glared at Mildred. She flinched under the full weight of his stare. He was enormous. Terrifying.

"There is a traditional method," he growled. "To test one of questionable blood."

Topaz groaned. "Oh, please, not . . ."

King Bluebeard marched to the door and flung it open.

"FETCH TWO HUNDRED MATTRESSES!" he bellowed.

Chapter 22
Princess Pyrite

"No problem," Topaz said confidently. "We can handle this."

Mildred stared at the tower of mattresses in horror. For one thing, they were filled with gravel, not straw. And what clueless person had started the rumor that her mattress should turn into gold if she slept on it?

"I mean, you only have to sleep on a few dozen," Topaz went on. "Father couldn't find enough gravel to fill two hundred. That reduces your chances of slipping dramatically."

And those silk sheets were just adding insult to injury.

"How am I supposed to sleep on gravel without bruising?" Mildred protested. "It's not like I'm an earth witch."

Topaz shrugged. "Add cushioning."

"I'm not allowed to use cushioning!"

Topaz rolled her eyes. "Well, if you're going to insist on following the *rules* . . ."

Two trumpets called a fanfare as the king marched out towards them. The courtyard filled as courtiers and servants poured out behind him, looking eager for the spectacle.

"Isn't my idea magnificent?" he called. "The only way to test the blood of a true princess. Now we shall disprove the claim of this pretender once and for all!"

Mildred felt like hiding.

"Magnificent," Topaz muttered. "That's one word for it. Another would be 'moronic.'"

"What's wrong, dear daughter?" the king smirked, turning to her. "There's no chance to cheat now, wouldn't you say?"

"There's no chance to *pass*," Topaz retorted. "This isn't the tradition! Those are supposed to be feather mattresses, not gravel. And she's supposed to bruise because you put one teensy, tiny vegetable underneath. What were you *thinking?*"

"I was thinking that my blood would show strength, not delicacy."

"That's the *opposite* of the tradition!"

"Regardless," the king growled, "I'm confident this will prove things."

"How?" Topaz demanded. "This is the most ridiculous idea I've ever heard. One visit to Byrina is all it would take —"

"Magic is untrustworthy!" the king snarled.

"And mattresses are *better?*"

"I'll do it!" Mildred cried. "I'll do it! Just stop fighting!"

Topaz gave her a look of exasperation.

King Bluebeard gestured for a servant. A burly man pushed through the crowd, dragging a tall ladder. He pushed it against the gravel mattresses with a *thump*.

The king smirked. "Go on," he said. "Prove your story."

Hating the attention, Mildred climbed up the ladder with wobbly legs. As she perched on the top, rocks already digging into her thighs, the burly servant pulled the ladder away.

"Sleep well tonight!" the king laughed. "And try not to fall off. Then we'll see if you can really be who you claim!"

He marched out of the courtyard, half the courtiers following him. Two trumpeters let out a loud fanfare, proclaiming his exit, as they trailed in the king's wake.

Mildred stared down at the remaining audience in misery. She did not see why her father had decided to make this such a public thing. It seemed pointlessly nasty.

Topaz flung her arms back in despair. "I can't do anything to save you, Mildred. Only the truth can do that now."

Mildred stared at her. *Has she gone crazy?*

"Come," Topaz said mournfully to the rest of the courtiers. "Let us leave her and return first thing in the morning."

Nodding and murmuring, most of the finely-dressed courtiers

disappeared back into the castle with her. After a few minutes, the rest looked bored and left, too. Now, only the servants and guards remained.

Mildred pressed her cheek against the relatively flat spot she'd found and stared out at the pink-and-orange sunset.

This is so unfair, she thought. *What does he think this will accomplish? Why would this sort of test prove anything?*

Of course she was bruised in the morning. Mildred felt numb as the servants inspected her. One more home where she wouldn't be welcome. One more family she was going to have to leave.

"Just as one would expect," one servant woman announced. "Bruised from head to foot."

"So?" Topaz demanded. "I would be, too, if I had slept on gravel!"

"Check the mattress," the king growled.

Looking baffled, the nearest servant nodded. He walked over to the mattress, slit it open, and emptied it.

Gasps ran across the courtyard. Gold nuggets tumbled out in every direction.

"Gold," King Bluebeard rumbled. "Just as the rumors have said. Only a princess could do this."

"Wait!" one courtier cried, holding up a nugget. "This is just fools' gold! Nothing valuable about it!"

Irritation flashed in the king's eyes.

"Fools' gold?" Topaz gasped, diving to the ground to examine the nuggets. "Dad, tell them what you were planning to name your second daughter, if you ever had one!"

"Carbuncle."

Topaz shot him an angry look.

The king's face colored. "Or . . . er . . . Pyrite?"

"You see?" Topaz shouted. "Fools' gold makes only further proof. This is Princess Pyrite!"

"Pyrite," the servants chanted, looking eager to earn favor. "Pyrite."

"Wait a minute," Mildred protested. "That's not —"

"Shut up," Topaz muttered, flinging an arm around her and waving at everybody. "Now smile and wave."

"Father wanted to keep his options open," Topaz explained. They were in her private rooms, which she had locked to keep out curious servants who kept trying to peek at them. "This way, if you proved to be a liar, he could still reject you. He can be a little bit weasely that way. But I think your behavior impressed him."

"Why?" Mildred asked slowly. "I didn't do anything."

"Precisely." Topaz ticked off points on her fingers. "You didn't cry. You didn't scream. You didn't whine. You didn't run. You didn't try to bribe the guards. You didn't hide your bruises. You didn't even try to rationalize them. In fact, you pretty much behaved better in every way than I would have, in your place." She grinned mischievously.

Mildred stared at her.

"Frankly, you'll make a much better princess than me. You'd just be useless as a queen."

Mildred wasn't sure if she felt relieved or insulted by this.

Topaz yawned and stretched. "Anyway, he made me stay up all night looking through our family paintings. You resemble Great-Great-Grandma Opal, in case you're interested. And you look slightly like Great-Uncle Tidy."

"Tidy?" Mildred repeated, startled.

"Our princes are called after virtues. You would have been named 'Punctual,' if you were a boy."

"'Thurgold' isn't —"

"Dad's parents named him 'Thrifty.' He changed it when he became king." Topaz paused. "Come to think of it, he might hate that even more than the nicknames I give him!"

The next three days were divided between numerous declarations, three banquets, five decorators wanting to design her personal rooms, eight bodyguards, six dressmakers, and one odious shoemaker.

She hated the shoemaker.

"See?" the man cried, flourishing his latest design. It featured laces that crisscrossed all the way up to the knees, diamond buttons shaped like flowers, and the tallest pair of heels she had ever seen. "What do you think?"

Mildred blanched.

"See how only the finest materials are used here, and here —"

"I'd like something simpler. That I can walk in."

"Your highness pleases to joke!" The shoemaker chortled. "Everyone knows shoes are not meant for walking, but for decorating the feet!"

"And *walking*."

"Nonsense," the shoemaker sniffed. "A simpler design would be beneath my elves."

Mildred stared in bafflement at her sister.

"Tiny creatures that sneak in and do all his work for him while he's asleep," Topaz whispered. "Don't ask. They're not real. He's just insane."

Mildred backed away.

It took nearly a week before Mildred found time to slip away from her bodyguards and turn back the frog marquess. Then she made the mistake of telling Topaz in front of their father.

He exploded with rage.

"No daughter of mine uses magic!" he screamed at her. "*Ever!*"

Mildred gaped at him. "But — somebody needed —"

"*Ever!*"

"Don't be so unreasonable, Father," Topaz snapped. "What were we supposed to do, keep the frog forever?"

"I-it's not like I did anything bad," Mildred quavered. "I just wanted to —"

"If I ever catch you using magic again, you'll be *banished from the kingdom!*"

The king stormed out of the room and slammed the door behind him. Two trumpets fanfared and followed him down the hallway.

Mildred collapsed down on Topaz's couch. Her eyes were wide, and she was shaking.

"Not ever?" she whispered. She felt a sense of loss so deep, words couldn't contain it. "Not *ever?*"

"So immature," Topaz growled.

"How can he demand that?" Mildred whispered. "Magic is . . . part of who I am."

Topaz sighed. "So just don't tell him when you use it. Sneak behind his back. I'll cover for you."

Mildred squeezed her eyes shut. *I don't want to sneak behind his back. I want my family to accept me. Why can't he do that? Why won't he just accept me?*

That was the night Aunt Oplisa came.

Chapter 23
An Unwelcome Visitor

"**P**yrite**,**" the voice spat. "What a fitting name for one who gives up power for frippery."

Mildred stared at the window, her mouth dry as ash. She had just pulled on her nightgown, turned around, and found — this.

Aunt Oplisa stood on the windowsill, broomstick in hand. A full moon glowed behind her, illuminating the all-gingham guest room.

"Aunt Oplisa," she whispered. "What are you doing here?"

"What am *I* doing here?" Aunt Oplisa flung her broomstick down on the floor. "What are *you* doing here?"

"M-my father lives here," Mildred stammered. "I got kicked out of the Academy. So I —"

"So you came to claim his wealth?" Aunt Oplisa said icily. "You came to claim that paltry Normal's influence? Drakin would *never* have —"

"Drakin *did!*" Mildred shot back angrily. "That's why I *exist!*"

Aunt Oplisa squeezed her fist around a vase of flowers. It crumpled, spraying water across the floor. The droplets spattered in a perfectly even pattern across her indigo cloak.

"Drakin would never give up so easily," she hissed.

Mildred swallowed. Her aunt had a point. But she hadn't chosen to go to the Academy in the first place.

"Aunt Oplisa," Mildred started hesitantly. "I —"

"And now you're living with *Normals!*" Aunt Oplisa screamed. "You're supposed to dominate trash, not live with it!"

Mildred shut her mouth. Her aunt would not understand.

"Still, it's not too late to redeem yourself." Aunt Oplisa's voice quieted. "There has never been a better time to kill your death-enemy. I know where Horinwa and his daughter live. Anklistine can brew a poison that fire witches are especially susceptible to —"

"I don't want to kill Rulisa!" Mildred burst out.

Aunt Oplisa pulled back, her eyes narrowing. "Don't be so short-sighted, Drakin's daughter. Death-enemies can be replaced. I've killed seven in my lifetime."

Mildred clenched her fists. Why did everyone assume she only wanted Rulisa alive to keep an enemy?

"Fine," Aunt Oplisa sighed. "I suppose we could slaughter your Normal relations instead. Hardly worth the effort, but you could always follow through the rest of Drakin's plan to take over the Four Kingdoms. If you simply must surround yourself with this tawdriness —"

"Stay away from my family!" Mildred shrieked.

Aunt Oplisa's eyebrows lowered.

"Family?" she asked quietly. "We are your family. Those things are beyond your contempt. Drakin knew that."

"Get out," Mildred hissed, seizing a gingham pillow. "Don't ever come back. I'll — I'll kill you if you hurt them. And I know you wouldn't want to harm me."

Silence fell.

Aunt Oplisa sighed, reaching for a pocket. "Well, of course I would rather not, but I can't have you defying me."

Mildred's eyes widened. She pinched the air and started chanting hastily.

Aunt Oplisa laughed, with neither malice nor humor. "You know so little, Drakin's daughter. You are replaceable. Quite a bother, having to deal with a small child again, but still replaceable."

Mildred clenched her fists. "You can't kill me," she said, her voice shaking. "I'm good at wards."

"Oh, Drakin's daughter," Aunt Oplisa sighed. She seemed genuinely regretful. "You know so little." She pulled a small white stone out of her pocket and tossed it.

Mildred watched it arc towards her. *What . . .?* she wondered.

Then her wards exploded.

Wind-stone! Mildred gasped, clutching her throat. She couldn't breathe!

"Your mother specialized in manipulation," Aunt Oplisa murmured, looking out the open window. "I do not. I simply turn a witch's magic against herself."

Mildred fell to the floor, her lungs burning. *Need . . . air!* she wanted to scream.

"And now I'll have to let a suitable man in the manor," Aunt Oplisa sighed. "That, or allow Lilith out to find one. What a *bother* this is."

Mildred clawed at her neck. The wind-stone had embedded itself there. Her fingers touched the thin chain that hung underneath her billowing nightgown.

Mildred seized it, fumbling for the tiny gold disc.

Save me! she cried silently. *Please!*

"Didn't Anklistine once want to marry?" Aunt Oplisa mused, running her fingers along the broomstick handle. "Oh, but of course — I had to kill him. He challenged my authority."

Save me, Mildred pleaded, clutching the talisman. *Save me — now — please!*

The wind-stone made a sharp popping noise. It clicked to the floor. Mildred lunged forward, gasping for breath.

"Hmm?" Aunt Oplisa muttered, turning around. "What did —"

A wall of fire exploded up from her feet. Aunt Oplisa shrieked for a split second before flames engulfed her in a cage.

"*Mildred is not replaceable!*" Aunt Lilith roared.

"Aunt Lilith!" Mildred gasped. "Aunt — Oplisa! Is she —?"

"Not dead." Aunt Hurda grunted with effort as she heaved herself over the windowsill. She pulled a broomstick up with her. "Captured. Soundproof. Hee hee."

"Though I wouldn't weep if she were," Aunt Anklistine muttered, stepping off her own broomstick and into the room. "Three fire witches had better be enough to hold her."

"Three?" Mildred repeated numbly.

Someone flung a struggling sack into the room, then climbed up after the rest of them.

"What's the gingerbread witch doing here?" Mildred cried. Her mind caught up with her. "Wait . . . what are *you* doing here? You're supposed to be cursed!"

"Not much longer," Aunt Hurda smirked.

The gingerbread witch dragged the sack across the floor. She spat at the flames. "Killed my brother, didn't you? Wouldn't mind a much more vicious revenge."

"Leenon," Aunt Anklistine said chillingly.

The gingerbread witch grumbled and dumped out the sack. Out fell an angry, scarred, and no-longer-quite-so-skinny girl.

"Cabbage!" Mildred cried. "What's she doing here?"

Aunt Hurda grinned, showing beautiful white teeth. She'd apparently forgotten to make them look black this morning. "Breaker."

"Beauty," the girl snarled rebelliously. "I have a name."

Mildred's eyes widened. She'd done an extra-credit assignment on Breakers.

"Don't kill the Normal!" she gasped. "You can't —"

"Oh, hush," Aunt Anklistine muttered, tracing out a line of dirt with her foot. "Breakers are a conduit. One only has to kill them if one wants to destroy a curse."

"And we'd much rather transfer it," Aunt Hurda said smugly.

"Let's hurry up," Aunt Lilith said, looking worried. "There's not much time before the spell moves back into us."

The gingerbread witch nodded and wrestled Cabbage next to the cage.

Aunt Anklistine reached for Aunt Hurda. Aunt Lilith touched Aunt Anklistine. Aunt Hurda stepped on Aunt Lilith's foot. The gingerbread witch shoved Cabbage's hand into the cage.

"Yeouch!" she screamed.

"Transfer," the gingerbread witch growled.

Lightning shot from Cabbage, back at the aunts, through the gingerbread witch, then straight into the flames. The fire extinguished just in time to hear Aunt Oplisa's scream.

"Hurts, does it?" the gingerbread witch asked eagerly.

"The compulsion should kick in next," Aunt Lilith murmured.

Aunt Oplisa snarled and screamed and gnashed her teeth. She fought to keep from moving, fought to raise her arms to strike her sisters. But neither, it seemed, were possible.

"Broomstick," Aunt Hurda smirked, holding up her twiggy shambles, "take that water witch back to Ebony Drake. No detours, no stops, no deceleration. Oh, and make it really unpleasantly bumpy."

The broom shot from her hand and smacked Aunt Oplisa off her feet. Seconds later, it was zooming out the window with her.

"Have a horrible flight!" Aunt Hurda called, waving.

Mildred ran out the window to watch Aunt Oplisa leaving.

"How come you didn't do that years ago?" she whispered.

"Because we couldn't invite people into the manor ourselves," Aunt Lilith said darkly. "Part of Oplisa's curse."

"And it takes an outside witch to transfer curses," the gingerbread witch added, clapping her hands with glee.

"Thank you, Leenon," Aunt Anklistine said shortly. "It doesn't bring back Tamarn, but it's something. At least now, she will be forced to live alone with no one to impress, control, or master."

The gingerbread witch snorted, as if this were not enough. But she looked reasonably pleased.

Cabbage was staring at her hands, her eyes wide. "What'd you d-do?" she stammered. "I f-felt all tingly."

"You have no magic," Aunt Anklistine explained distractedly. "That meant you were empty. We stored a spell in you."

Cabbage's mouth opened and closed.

"Now you can go," Aunt Anklistine added, pointing. "We're done with you."

"I want payment," Cabbage said immediately. "You kept me prisoner for weeks."

Aunt Lilith stared at her in exasperation.

"We could've left you for Oplisa," Hurda growled. "She was going to kill you to break wards around the home of her latest enemy."

Cabbage just stared at them flintily.

"Here," Mildred said. She ran over to her jewelry box, which was stuffed with trinkets from her sister. "Take one of these."

Cabbage ran her fingers through them, eyes lit with greed. She reached out and snatched three.

"Out," Aunt Anklistine ordered, pointing.

Cabbage sniffed and marched out Mildred's door. There was a *thump*.

An Unwelcome Visitor

Mildred started and then ran after her.

"It's okay!" she shouted to the guards outside her room. "I gave her those! She isn't a thief!"

"We're gonna have to make plans," Aunt Hurda growled. "Oplisa has allies."

"Later," Aunt Lilith sighed. "Right now, we need to discuss our niece."

The king did not look impressed to be awoken so early in the morning. And when Mildred introduced him to Aunt Anklistine, his eyes opened in rage.

"*You!*"

"Love the blue hair," Aunt Anklistine said coolly. "Ready to apologize for your insult yet?"

"Fetch my daughter," the king snarled to a passing servant.

The man started. "Er! Your majesty — erm —" He looked, confused, at Mildred.

"The other one, you dolt!" the king roared.

"Yes, your majesty!" The servant bowed and scurried away.

Mildred looked around the king's bedchamber, decorated in silver and gold filigree. She watched Aunt Hurda pull a spiderweb from her pocket and tangle it in the nearest draperies. King Bluebeard continued to glare at Aunt Anklistine, who ignored him. Aunt Lilith stood in a corner, looking tense as she scrubbed the doorframe.

Topaz stumbled into the room, her hair a mess and her nightgown knocked askew. "Whassit?" she mumbled. "Too early."

"Come in," the king growled. "We apparently have something to discuss with — these."

Topaz cracked an eye open, peering at Aunt Hurda. She cracked the other open, peering at Mildred. Then she looked back at Aunt Hurda, busily rubbing dirt into striped gold filigree.

"Your aunts, I presume?" she mumbled.

Mildred nodded.

"Figures." Topaz flumped onto the chair by her father's bed. "They're even uglier than my Aunt Lancie."

Aunt Lilith stiffened. Aunt Hurda grinned, looking pleased.

"So?" Topaz yawned. "Whassit? Something about Mildred?"

"Yes," Aunt Lilith said immediately. "She can't stay here."

"Of course she can!" King Bluebeard snarled. "She's my daughter!"

"You never deserved our sister," Aunt Anklistine snorted. "You certainly can't have our niece. Your paltry offerings mean nothing."

Mildred swallowed. She opened her mouth to speak.

"Paltry?" the king roared. "I rule one of the Four Kingdoms! I have the most wealth in Restva! And you call that *paltry?*"

"You have no magic, and you won't allow our niece to use hers either," Aunt Anklistine retorted. "That is paltry indeed."

"She's my daughter," the king snarled. "She's only your niece."

Aunt Lilith's eyes flashed. "And yet, we raised her."

"Only because you *stole* her from me!"

"No, Drakin stole her," Aunt Anklistine said coldly. "We simply fulfilled her wish to keep you away."

Thurgold's red face darkened with rage.

Mildred gulped, shrinking back against her chair.

"I am king here," Thurgold snarled. "Don't forget that."

"Wouldn't be if other kings didn't protect you," Aunt Hurda grunted. She opened a chest-of-drawers, pulled out a handful of undergarments, and tossed them under the bed. "If they didn't have witch allies, you'd be dead long over."

"What's so wrong with Mildred staying here, anyway?" Topaz protested. "She's happy, isn't she?"

"Mildred needs an education," Aunt Lilith said firmly. "Would Thurgold —"

"Bluebeard," Topaz put in.

"Fine. Would Bluebeard allow Mildred to practice her magic here?"

The king glowered. His expression made it clear he would not.

"So, we need to find a good school," Aunt Anklistine said briskly. "Cyclone Institute might take her, despite the disaster at Smoldering. The Sukanil School of Magic Studies isn't a bad option, either."

"There's another option," Aunt Lilith added quietly. "I don't think school is necessary. Anklistine once taught at Hemlock. I know a great deal, too. We can manage without sending you away."

"Then . . . couldn't you . . ." Mildred swallowed. "Couldn't you just come to stay here? Can't I just live with *all* of you?"

The king's face mottled with rage.

"Live here?" Aunt Anklistine asked scornfully. She looked around the room with disdain. "There are no defenses against witches. It's secure against invasion, but hardly a determined death-enemy. Not to mention decor . . ." She sniffed.

"Too clean," Aunt Hurda nodded.

"Too chaotic," Aunt Lilith shuddered, wrinkling her nose.

"Get out," the king growled, rising to his feet. "I've put up with this talk far too long. You have never been welcome here."

"Do you want me to curse your hair another color?" Aunt Anklistine purred. "Maybe greenish-pink?"

Topaz choked back a guffaw.

"Think it should be her decision," Aunt Hurda grunted, pointing at Mildred. "Make her pick."

Everyone focused on Mildred. She shrank back.

"Well?" Aunt Lilith demanded. Her voice was gentle, but her eyes sharp. "Which do you want? Which family?"

"I . . . I . . ." Mildred's mouth opened. *I can't do this! I can't choose between them! How can they make me pick?*

Topaz yawned. "Why don't you just send her to White Magic Academy?"

There was a short silence.

"White —?" Mildred gasped.

"That's *not* an option," Aunt Lilith said frigidly. "It's a laughingstock. No academic standards whatsoever. They might have fairly decent security —"

"NO!" King Thurgold shouted.

"It's quite respected in Byrina, actually," Aunt Anklistine murmured, looking thoughtful. "And they specialize in training bodyguards for royalty. Might solve some of this thing's problems." She wiggled her fingers at the king.

"ABSOLUTELY NOT!" King Bluebeard shouted.

"I like visiting Byrina," Topaz said brightly. "King Horan's sons are quite good-looking."

"THIS SUBJECT IS NOW CLOSED! I FORBID IT!"

"Oh, shut up," Aunt Anklistine muttered, flinging her fingers in his direction.

King Thurgold's beard wove across his face, sealing his mouth shut. His face turned crimson. "MMMFFHH! MMFHHHHH MFMFH!"

"Why hasn't anybody ever mentioned this existed before?" Mildred whispered. "No one ever thought I ought to know this?"

"I figured you already knew," Topaz shrugged.

"We never mentioned it," Aunt Lilith said heatedly, "because it's irrelevant. Been around for less than sixty years. It's worthless."

"Oplisa would hate it," Aunt Hurda cackled. "I like the idea."

"They're supposed to be quite good with defense," Aunt Anklistine mused. "That might be good for our niece. She's useless at fighting."

"White Magic Academy," Mildred said slowly. "White . . . Magic . . . Academy . . ."

She couldn't believe no one had ever told her it existed. It sounded idyllic. Perfect. Like a dream.

"All right," Aunt Anklistine said, standing. "That school would be acceptable to me."

"Me too," Aunt Hurda grinned.

Mildred looked over at Aunt Lilith. She seemed to be fuming.

"You go with her," Aunt Anklistine directed. "Make sure they don't corrupt her too badly."

Aunt Lilith's look of frustration faded. She nodded, jerkily.

White Magic Academy, Mildred thought. *White magic . . .*

A huge smile spread across her face.

White magic that a school would actually *teach!*

Chapter 24

Finally . . .

Under the pale moon, the building glittered. It was shaped from transparent quartz, covered in hexagonal spikes, and it looked like it was growing.

"It's beautiful," Mildred whispered dreamily. She barely even noticed she was sitting on a broomstick.

"Mm," Aunt Lilith muttered.

Mildred closed her eyes, basking in the feeling of contentment.

King Bluebeard had not improved his attitude towards her going. In fact, he'd been so angry, he had barely spoken two words for the rest of the week.

"But I can make him change his mind eventually," Topaz whispered, hugging her as Aunt Lilith prepared the broomsticks. "King Horan sends his sons there to learn theory. And Dad really needs to learn to stop antagonizing people just as powerful as he is."

"I'll miss you," Mildred sniffed. "I've never had a sister before."

Topaz laughed. "And where do you think I'm going to run first, from now on, whenever Dad drives me crazy?"

Mildred opened her eyes, watching the building. *I should invite Trasia to join me. Maybe I could even convince Rulisa!*

Stranger things had happened, after all.

From now on, everything was going to be perfect.

Black Magic Academy

Deadly Spells	Old Tongue	Unraveling	Traditions
Disagreeable Spells	Old Tongue Fundamentals	Fundamental Unraveling	Fundamental Traditions
Menacing Spells	Old Tongue Basics	Rudimentary Unraveling	Basic Traditions
Frightening Spells	Old Tongue Speaking	Basic Unraveling	Academy Traditions
Aggressive Spells	Old Tongue Writing	Intermediate Unraveling	Intermediate Traditions
Deceptive Spells	Old Tongue Grammar	Elemental Unraveling	Restvanian Traditions
Vicious Spells	Old Tongue Spelling	Advanced Unraveling	Political Traditions
Merciless Spells	Old Tongue Vocabulary	Expert Unraveling	Advanced Traditions
Malignant Spells	Old Tongue Singing	Talisman Unraveling	Contemporary Traditions
Virulent Spells	Old Tongue Chanting	Preventative Unraveling	Expert Traditions
Destructive Spells	Old Tongue Composing	Unraveled Unraveling	Malevolent Traditions
Treacherous Spells	Old Tongue Proficiency	Imperceptible Unraveling	Transformative Traditions
Coercive Spells	Old Tongue Spellcrafting	Transferable Unraveling	Manipulative Traditions
Deadly Spells	Old Tongue Fluency	White Magic Unraveling	Death-Enemy Traditions

Classes Taught

Cauldron	Elements	Witch History	Talismans
Cauldron Fundamentals	Fundamental Elements	Current Events	Fundamental Talismans
Cauldron Usages	Basic Elements	Basic Witch History	Talismans and Charms
Basic Brews	Intermediate Elements	Intermediate Witch History	Basic Talismans
Cauldron Cleansing	Summoning Elements	Advanced Witch History	Talismans and Baubles
Intermediate Brews	Elemental Theory	Expert Witch History	Intermediate Talismans
Advanced Brews	Advanced Elements	Historical Curses	Talismans and Amulets
Cauldron Cooking	Expert Elements	History of Metamorphosis	Advanced Talismans
Expert Brews	Elemental Protection	History of the Institutes	Repairing Talismans
Poisonous Brews	Elemental Illusion	History of the Four Kingdoms	Defensive Talismans
Elemental Brews	Elemental Conflict	History of Superiority	Expert Talismans
Undectable Brews	Elemental Strengthening	Historical Death-Enemies	Destructive Talismans
Alchemy	Elemental Reversal	History of the Forest Beyond	Permanent Talismans
Exilirs	Elemental Command	History of the Academy	Familiar Talismans

About the Author

Emily Martha Sorensen has always loved fantasy. Growing up, she would devour the works of C. S. Lewis, Michael Ende, Diana Wynne Jones, and Patricia C. Wrede. She loves humor, and she has a particular fondness for fairy tale retellings.

She wrote her first book at ten years old, after deciding that she wanted to write professionally at the age of six. She completed her first draft of this book at fifteen, and has gone through several dozen rewrites since then.

She has a husband named Ben, who also writes, and a fifteen-month-old daughter named Wednesday. They currently reside in Provo, Utah.

You can read more about her, or find more of her stories, at http://www.emilymarthasorensen.com.

CPSIA information can be obtained
at www.ICGtesting.com
Printed in the USA
BVHW080940140620
581357BV00003B/123